T0137515

THE GREAT SIGN

THE KEY TO UNLOCKING BIBLICAL END TIMES PROPHECY, THE RAPTURE OF THE CHURCH, AND TRIBULATION PERIOD

Putting the Four Blood Moons and God's Festivals in Context

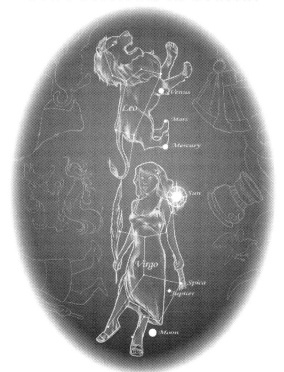

JAMES L. KOONTZ

WESTBOW
PRESS
A DIVISION OF THOMAS NELSON
& ZONDERVAN

Scripture taken from the New King James Version. Copyright © 1979, 1980, 1982 by Thomas Nelson, Inc. Used by permission. All rights reserved.

WestBow Press books may be ordered through booksellers or by contacting:

WestBow Press
A Division of Thomas Nelson & Zondervan
1663 Liberty Drive
Bloomington, IN 47403
www.westbowpress.com
1 (866) 928-1240

ISBN: 978-1-4908-4563-0 (sc)
ISBN: 978-1-4908-4565-4 (hc)
ISBN: 978-1-4908-4564-7 (e)

Library of Congress Control Number: 2014913077

Printed in the United States of America.

WestBow Press rev. date: 9/2/2014

This book is dedicated to my younger brother, Richard, and my beloved children, James, Ronnie, and Joseph.

Introduction

AN EXCITING TIME TO BE ALIVE

I became a Christian in Rio Vista, California, through my pastor's son, Glenn. I am forever thankful to Glenn for having the courage to bring me to the saving knowledge of Jesus Christ. From then on I studied Bible prophecy, describing myself as a Watchman on the Wall, studying and trying to discern what the Holy Spirit would have me learn, searching out those things God has hidden. During the past roughly forty years, I have read many books written by Hal Lindsey, Tim LaHaye, the late Pastor Chuck Smith, Pastor John Hagee, and Evangelist Perry Stone, just to name a few. I could not get enough of Bible prophecy as it applied to the time I am living in. Then along came the Internet and the World Wide Web, which became a powerful tool for research, viewing videos, and talking with other Christians concerning prophecy about the end times. As a result of all of these factors, I offer to Christians

1

and non-Christians alike what the Holy Spirit has led me to discern and subsequently reveal through reading, studying, and reaching out to my Christian brothers and sisters. This is an exciting time to be alive as we move ever closer to the rapture of the church or the bride of Christ (Ephesians 5:25–32; Revelation 19:7–9 NKJV) and the subsequent beginning of the seven-year tribulation, the ending of which heralds the second coming of Jesus Christ.

Both Christians and non-Christians who are seeking to understand the exciting time in which we live have no further to look than to Jesus speaking to His disciples about the end times. Jesus spoke of many signs that would portend the coming end to the age of grace: wars and commotions; nations rising against nations, and kingdoms against kingdoms; great earthquakes in various places; famines and pestilences; fearful sights and great signs from heaven (Luke 21: 9–11).

This book will discuss the signs in the heavens, concentrating on the four blood moons, the solar eclipse, and the great sign in Revelation 12:1. Setting the stage is Chapter 1, which examines the spring and fall feasts. This discussion of the spring feasts and the day of Pentecost sets the foundation for prophetic fulfillment of the Lord's fall feasts. This is not meant to be a comprehensive discussion of the feasts, but a simple and effective summary, showing Christ's fulfillment of the spring feasts and leading to the idea that if Christ fulfilled the spring feasts, it is logical to believe that He will also fulfill the fall feasts.

Chapter 2 discusses the rapture of the Church, and Chapter 3 discusses the rapture of the church in context with the Feast of Trumpets. Chapter 4 explores the term "twinkling of an eye," and Chapter 5 discusses the three previous blood moon tetrads in history and the upcoming tetrad (beginning on April 15, 2014) with regard to Jewish history and how they relate to present time. Chapter 6 explores the chronological nature of the book of Revelation. Chapter 7 discusses the great sign, the key to unlocking the biblical End Times, including the approximate timing of the rapture of the church (also known as the bride of Christ) and the dates of the tribulation period, respectively. Chapter 8 briefly examines the Mazzaroth detailing God's redemptive plan for humankind in the heavens. Chapter 9 discusses Bible prophecy as it relates to Christ's birth, death, and resurrection, looking forward to why God and His Son want us to know the timing of the rapture and Christ's second coming. Chapter 10 puts all the pieces together. Chapter 11 discusses my responsibility as a Watchman on the Wall. Chapter 12 asks you, the reader, what do you do now that you know that Christ's return is imminent. What should you do next, now that you are aware of the signs of the times, heralding one of the most exciting times in world history besides Christ walking on this earth— the rapture of His bride.

So let's examine the exciting time in which we are living by looking back in world history when Jesus fulfilled His Father's divine appointed times or appointments, also known as the Lord's festivals or feasts.

Chapter 1

The Lord's Feasts, Festivals, Appointed Times or Divine Appointments—The Spring and Fall Feasts

D esiring to gain a greater understanding of The Old and New Testament and to know God more fully, I began studying the Lord's feasts (Leviticus 23:2, 4) after hearing about the upcoming four blood moons and the Jewish lunar calendar. Up until then, I had been concentrating almost entirely on the Western view of prophecy, as if the Western view of prophecy was all about us rather than about God and the Jewish people. I also desired to know how the feast days possibly fit in to Bible prophecy, if they did at all.

I now believe that the Lord's feast days are pivotal to understanding Bible prophecy. Based on the evidence, I believe Christ fulfilled all of the spring feasts, setting the stage for Him to fulfill God's fall feasts. Paul says it best in Colossians, that the feasts are but a shadow of things to come (Colossians 2:16–17). He knew Christ would fulfill the feasts as the feasts were a foreshadowing of Christ's death (Passover), burial (Feast of Unleavened Bread), and resurrection (Feast of Firstfruits), fulfilling the spring feasts exactly on time. He fulfilled the Feast of Weeks (day of Pentecost) when He imbued His disciples with the Holy Spirit. Speaking of foreshadowing, it's interesting to note that in the Bible that all of the feasts are referred to as holy convocations. So, what is a convocation? In Hebrew, the word for *convocation* is *miqra'* (pronounced: mik-raw'), meaning *rehearsal*.[1] The logical question, then, before we discuss the feasts is, what are the Jewish people rehearsing? They were historically rehearsing the main event for each feast that Christ would ultimately prophetically fulfill as detailed in the chart below.[2]

[1] *Yahweh Restoration Ministry*. (2014, February 5). Retrieved from Bible Study Resources Strong's Concordance with Hebrew and Greek Lexicon searches: http://www.yrm.org/strongs/4744

[2] Chumney, E. (2014, 02 8). *Friends of Sabbath*. Retrieved from Friends of Sabbath: http://www.friendsofsabbath.org/Further_Research/Holy%20Days/The-Seven-Festivals-of-the-Messiah.pdf/Pages 24-25

Feast	Historical Aspect	Messianic Fulfillment
1. Passover (Pesach)	Israel's deliverance out of Egyptian bondage	Jesus' Death on the cross
2. Unleavened Bread (Hag HaMatzah)	Going out of Egypt	Jesus' Burial
3. First Fruits (Bikkurim)	Crossing Red Sea	Jesus' Resurrection
4. Pentecost (Shavuot)	Giving Torah at Mount Sinai	Pouring out of Holy Spirit
5. Rosh Hashanah or Feast of Trumpets	Blowing the Shofar/Jewish New Year	Resurrection of Dead/(Yom Teruah) Rapture (Natzal) of believers
6. Day of Atonement (Yom Kippur)	Priest entered the Holy of Holies Cleansing of the people's sin	The Day of Messiah's Second Coming
7. Tabernacles (Tabernacles)	Entering the Promised Land/Great Rejoicing	The Messianic Era/Millennium

Before studying the feasts, I also wanted to examine what a Biblical feast is. The discussion concerning the Biblical feasts begins in Genesis when God created the sun, moon, and stars, dividing the day from the night, and letting them be for signs and seasons (Genesis 1:14–19).

For so many years, I believed as I was taught in the churches I attended that seasons meant spring, summer, fall, and winter. This is true in the sense that things in the Bible can have two different, but correct meanings[3], as there is an annual cyclical pattern of the wandering stars (planets) and the sun and the moon during the four seasons. However, *season* has another meaning. In Hebrew, *season* is called *mow`ed* (pronounced: mo-ade'), meaning an appointment (fixed time), a festival, a signal (as appointed beforehand), appointed sign or

---

[3] *Merriam-Webster*. (2014, February 5). Retrieved from http://www.merriam-webster.com/dictionary/dual?show=0&t=1391665023/duality

time, and a feast.[4] In other words, the Lord's feasts or festivals (called feasts from now on) are God's divine appointments on God's calendar. Any boss's calendar, if you will, dictates events with regard to day and time, and this is no different with God's calendar. God is in charge. God's feasts are God's divine appointments on God's divine calendar, dictating events on specific dates and times. These divine appointments are ones that we do not want to miss, especially the fall feasts, as these are yet to be fulfilled.

The Lord's feast days are divided between the spring and the fall. The spring feasts are the Feast of Passover, the Feast of Unleavened Bread, the Feast of Firstfruits, and Feast of Weeks or Pentecost. The fall feasts are the Feast of Trumpets, Yom Kippur or Day of Atonement, and the Feast of Tabernacles.

SPRING FEASTS
THE FEAST OF PASSOVER

The Feast of Passover began when God instructed the Israelites who were still in Egypt to slaughter a lamb or a goat and place the blood on their doorposts so that when God passed over their houses, God would

---

[4] *Yahweh Restoration Ministry.* (2014, February 5). Retrieved from Bible Study Resources Strong's Concordance with Hebrew and Greek Lexicon searches: http://www.yrm.org/strongs/4150

not kill the firstborn son inside. Of course this was God's response to the Pharaoh's edict that all Hebrew firstborn sons were to be killed.

This is the perfect picture of Christ shedding His blood for our sins on the cross. God will then pass over us as we are covered by His Son's blood. God no longer sees our sins as we have been bought with His Son's blood and are now His sons and daughters, having no fear of God's judgment.

The Lord's Feast of Passover is detailed in the following Old Testament verses:

> Now the Lord spoke to Moses and Aaron in the land of Egypt, saying, "This month shall be your beginning of months; it shall be the first month of the year to you. Speak to all the congregation of Israel, saying: 'On the tenth of this month every man shall take for himself a lamb, according to the house of his father, a lamb for a household. And if the household is too small for the lamb, let him and his neighbor next to his house take it according to the number of the persons; according to each man's need you shall make your count for the lamb. Your lamb shall be without blemish, a male of the first year. You may take it from the sheep or from the goats ... It is the Lord's Passover.'" (Exodus 12:1–11)

These are the Feasts of the Lord, holy convocations which you shall proclaim at their appointed times. On the fourteenth day of the first month at twilight is the Lord's Passover. (Leviticus 23:4–5)

The Lord's Feast of Passover was fulfilled by Christ by Christ dying on Passover and is detailed in the following New Testament verses:

When Pilate therefore heard that saying, he brought Jesus out and sat down in the judgment seat in a place that is called The Pavement, but in Hebrew, Gabbatha. Now it was the Preparation Day of the Passover ... Then he delivered Him to them to be crucified. So they took Jesus and led Him away. (John 19:13–16)

The next day John saw Jesus coming toward him, and said, "Behold! The Lamb of God who takes away the sin of the world!" (John 1:29)

Therefore purge out the old leaven, that you may be a new lump, since you truly are unleavened. For indeed Christ, our Passover, was sacrificed for us. (1 Corinthians 5:7)

Now it came to pass, when Jesus had finished all these sayings, that He said to His disciples, "You know that after two days is the Passover, and the

Son of Man will be delivered up to be crucified."
(Matthew 26:1–2)

Spring Feasts
The Feast of Unleavened Bread

The Feast of Unleavened Bread lasts seven days, immediately following Passover. During this time, no leaven was to be found in a Jewish home nor was any leavened bread to be eaten. Leaven is representative of sin. The Feast of Unleavened Bread speaks of Christ's sinless sacrifice in which he bore the sins of the world. Christ, our unleavened bread, was placed in the grave during the Feast of Unleavened Bread. Showing us mercy and love, The Son of Man who had no sin died for all mankind so that we would live forever with Him. This also reminds me of the lamb or goat that was slain during the Feast of Passover as the animal had to be without blemish, representing the Lamb of God, the sinless Lamb without blemish slain for our transgressions. The Feast of Unleavened Bread is denoted from the time Christ died until His resurrection.

The Lord's Feast of Unleavened Bread is detailed in the following Old Testament verse:

And on the fifteenth day of the same month is the Feast of Unleavened Bread to the Lord; seven days you must eat unleavened bread. On the first day you shall have a holy convocation; you shall do no customary work on it. But you shall offer an offering made by fire to the Lord for seven days. The seventh day shall be a holy convocation; you shall do no customary work on it. (Leviticus 23:6–8)

The Lord's Feast of Unleavened Bread was fulfilled by Christ with Christ's death, burial, and resurrection and is detailed in the following New Testament verses:

Now behold, there was a man named Joseph, a council member, a good and just man. He had not consented to their decision and deed. He was from Arimathea, a city of the Jews, who himself was also waiting for the kingdom of God. This man went to Pilate and asked for the body of Jesus. Then he took it down, wrapped it in linen, and laid it in a tomb that was hewn out of the rock, where no one had ever lain before. (Luke 23:50–53)

And Jesus said to them, "I am the bread of life. He who comes to Me shall never hunger, and he who believes in Me shall never thirst." (John 6:25)

Therefore let us keep the feast, not with old leaven, nor with the leaven of malice and wickedness, but with the unleavened bread of sincerity and truth. (1 Corinthians 5:8)

SPRING FEASTS
THE FEAST OF FIRSTFRUITS

The Feast of Firstfruits is a seven-day feast, beginning on the evening of the fifteenth of Nisan. The firstfruits were sheaves (ears of corn or barley), the first offerings of the harvest that were presented to the Lord. Christ rose from the dead, conquering death, hell, and the grave during the Feast of Firstfruits as Christ is the Firstfruit of the Christian harvest. A biblical harvest usually consisted of the firstfruits, main harvest, and the gleanings, which were left for the poor (Leviticus 23:22). This is analogous to Christ being the Firstfruits, raptured saints before the tribulation being the main harvest, and the tribulation saints being the gleanings, the leftover in the harvest field.

The Lord's Feast of Firstfruits is detailed in the following Old Testament verses:

And the Lord spoke to Moses, saying, "Speak to the children of Israel, and say to them: 'When you come into the land which I give to you, and reap its harvest, then you shall bring a sheaf of the firstfruits of your harvest to the priest. He shall wave the sheaf before the Lord, to be accepted on your behalf; on the day after the Sabbath the priest shall wave it. And you shall offer on that day, when you wave the sheaf, a male lamb of the first year, without blemish, as a burnt offering to the Lord. Its grain offering shall be two-tenths of an ephah of fine flour mixed with oil, an offering made by fire to the Lord, for a sweet aroma; and its drink offering shall be of wine, one-fourth of a hin ... it shall be a statute forever throughout your generations in all your dwellings.'" (Leviticus 23:9–14)

Also on the day of the firstfruits, when you bring a new grain offering to the Lord at your Feast of Weeks, you shall have a holy convocation. You shall do no customary work. (Numbers 28:26)

The Lord's Feast of Firstfruits was fulfilled by Christ and is detailed in the following New Testament passage:

But now Christ is risen from the dead, and has become the firstfruits of those who have fallen asleep. For since by man came death, by Man also came the resurrection of the dead. For as in Adam all die, even so in Christ all shall be made alive. But each one in his own order: Christ the firstfruits, afterward those who are Christ's at His coming. (1 Corinthians 15:20–23)

Spring Feasts
The Feast of Weeks or Pentecost

Jesus' disciples were baptized with the Holy Spirit from His Father exactly fifty days after Passover as Jesus promised in the feast known as Pentecost. Jesus tells His disciples that the gift of the Holy Spirit would be given to them, and He asks them to wait in Jerusalem until they received the baptism of the Holy Spirit from His Father (Acts 1:4–8). When the disciples had all gathered in one place, there was a sound from heaven like a mighty rushing wind, and each person there spoke in tongues after receiving the Holy Spirit and became witnesses for Christ, bringing over 3,000 people to Him (Acts 2:40).

The Lord's Feast of Weeks or Pentecost is detailed in the following Old Testament verses:

And you shall count for yourselves from the day after the Sabbath, from the day that you brought the sheaf of the wave offering: seven Sabbaths shall be completed. Count fifty days to the day after the seventh Sabbath; then you shall offer a new grain offering to the Lord. You shall bring from your dwellings two wave loaves of two-tenths of an *ephah*. They shall be of fine flour; they shall be baked with leaven. They are the firstfruits to the Lord. And you shall offer with the bread seven lambs of the first year, without blemish, one young bull, and two rams. They shall be as a burnt offering to the Lord, with their grain offering and their drink offerings, an offering made by fire for a sweet aroma to the Lord. Then you shall sacrifice one kid of the goats as a sin offering, and two male lambs of the first year as a sacrifice of a peace offering ... it is a holy convocation to you. You shall do no customary work on it. It shall be a statute forever in all your dwellings throughout your generations. (Leviticus 23:15–21)

The Lord's Feast of Weeks or Pentecost was fulfilled as Christ promised His disciples when they were imbued with the Holy Spirit, birthing the church. Jews and Gentiles became one in Christ by His Spirit as detailed in the following New Testament verses:

And being assembled together with them, He commanded them not to depart from Jerusalem, but to wait for the Promise of the Father, "which," He said, "you have heard from Me; for John truly baptized with water, but you shall be baptized

with the Holy Spirit not many days from now."
(Acts 1:4–5)

When the Day of Pentecost had fully come,
they were all with one accord in one place. And
suddenly there came a sound from heaven,
as of a rushing mighty wind, and it filled the
whole house where they were sitting. Then
there appeared to them divided tongues, as of
fire, and *one* sat upon each of them. And they
were all filled with the Holy Spirit and began
to speak with other tongues, as the Spirit gave
them utterance. (Acts 2:1–4)

FALL FEASTS
ROSH HASHANAH OR THE FEAST OF TRUMPETS

Rosh Hashanah or the Feast of Trumpets is a two-day
feast, marking a time of repentance and the beginning
of the new year. The Hebrew word *rosh* means "chief
or head"[5] and *shanah* means *year*.[6] "Rosh Hashanah is

---

[5] *Yahweh Restoration Ministry*. (2014, February 5). Retrieved from
Bible Study Resources Strong's Concordance with Hebrew and
Greek Lexicon searches: http://www.yrm.org/strongs/

[6] *Yahweh Restoration Ministry*. (2014, February 5). Retrieved from
Bible Study Resources Strong's Concordance with Hebrew and
Greek Lexicon searches: http://www.yrm.org/strongs/

thus the head of the year on the civil calendar and is also known as the birthday of the world since the world was created on this day" (Talmud, Rosh Hashanah 11a).[7] Unlike any other feast, Rosh Hashanah begins on the new moon and is two days long, ensuring everyone has the opportunity to be notified and able to participate across the nation of Israel and surrounding nations (Diaspora Jews) where some of the Israelites were dispersed. This practice of a two-day feast has continued to today for all Jews observing this feast whether they are inside or outside of Israel.

The Lord's Feast of Trumpets is detailed in the following Old Testament verses:

> Then the Lord spoke to Moses, saying, "Speak to the children of Israel, saying: 'In the seventh month, on the first day of the month, you shall have a sabbath-rest, a memorial of blowing of trumpets, a holy convocation. You shall do no customary work *on it*; and you shall offer an offering made by fire to the Lord.'" (Leviticus 23:23–25)

> And in the seventh month, on the first day of the month, you shall have a holy convocation. You

---

[7] Chumney, E. (2014, 02 8). *Friends of Sabbath*. Retrieved from Friends of Sabbath: http://www.friendsofsabbath.org/Further_Research/ Holy%20Days/The-Seven-Festivals-of-the-Messiah.pdf/Page 103

shall do no customary work. For you it is a day of blowing the trumpets. (Numbers 29:1)

The Feast of Trumpets has many different names, themes, and idioms that are listed below.[8] I will discuss in Chapter 3 the ones that typically are recognized and/or discussed within the Christian community when talking about the rapture of the bride of Christ. I have put these in bold type.

Repentance
Head of the Year
Day of Judgment
The Opening of the Gates
Coronation of the Messiah
Day of Remembrance or Memorial
The Day of the Awakening Blast
The Wedding Ceremony
The Resurrection of the Dead
The Last Trump
The Hidden Day or Day of Concealment
Time of Jacob's Trouble (Birth pangs of Messiah)

Again, all of these names, themes, and/or idioms

---

[8] Chumney, E. (2014, 02 8). *Friends of Sabbath*. Retrieved from Friends of Sabbath: http://www.friendsofsabbath.org/Further_Research/ Holy%20Days/The-Seven-Festivals-of-the-Messiah.pdf/Pages 102-103

pointing to the rapture of the church on the Feast of Trumpets will be discussed in more detail in Chapter 3.

Fall Feasts
Yom Kippur or Day of Atonement

Yom Kippur is the holiest day of the year for the Jewish people and concentrates on atonement and repentance. This holy day is customarily observed by the Jewish people with two days of fasting and prayer to "afflict the soul," atoning for the sins of the past year. It usually falls in September or October every year.

Yom Kippur is detailed in the following Old Testament verses:

> "This shall be an everlasting statute for you, to make atonement for the children of Israel, for all their sins, once a year." And he did as the Lord commanded Moses. (Leviticus 16:34)

> And the Lord spoke to Moses, saying: "Also the tenth day of this seventh month shall be   t h e Day of Atonement. It shall be a holy convocation for you; you shall afflict your souls, and offer an offering made by fire to the Lord. And you shall do no work on that same day, for it is the Day of Atonement, to make atonement for you before the Lord your God." (Leviticus 23:26–28)

On the tenth day of this seventh month you shall have a holy convocation. You shall afflict your souls; you shall not do any work. (Numbers 29:7)

Christ's future fulfillment of Yom Kippur is detailed in the following New Testament verses:

For I do not desire, brethren, that you should be ignorant of this mystery, lest you should be wise in your own opinion, that blindness in part has happened to Israel until the fullness of the Gentiles has come in. And so all Israel will be saved, as it is written: "The Deliverer will come out of Zion, and He will turn away ungodliness from Jacob; For this is My covenant with them, When I take away their sins." (Romans 11:25–27)

And in that day His feet will stand on the Mount of Olives, which faces Jerusalem on the east. And the Mount of Olives shall be split in two, from east to west, Making a very large valley; Half of the mountain shall move toward the north and half of it toward the south. (Zechariah 14:4)

When the Son of Man comes in His glory, and all the holy angels with Him, then He will sit on the throne of His glory. (Matthew 25:31)

FALL FEASTS
FEAST OF TABERNACLES

The Feast of Tabernacles or the Festival of Booths occurs for seven days in September or October every year. This is a holiday of rejoicing and celebration, which is in marked contrast to the repentance and afflicting of souls at Yom Kippur. During this feast God instructed the Jewish people to build temporary booths, representing their dwellings in the wilderness on the way out of Egypt to the Promised Land.

The Feast of Tabernacles is detailed in the following Old Testament verses:

Then the Lord spoke to Moses, saying, "Speak to the children of Israel, saying: 'The fifteenth day of this seventh month shall be the Feast of Tabernacles for seven days to the Lord. On the first day there shall be a holy convocation. You shall do no customary work on it. For seven days you shall offer an offering made by fire to the Lord. On the eighth day you shall have a holy convocation, and you shall offer an offering made by fire to the Lord. It is a sacred assembly, and you shall do no customary work on it.'" (Leviticus 23:33–36)

You shall observe the Feast of Tabernacles seven days, when you have gathered from your threshing floor and from your winepress. (Deuteronomy 16:13)

You shall dwell in booths for seven days. All who are native Israelites shall dwell in booths. (Leviticus 23:42)

Christ's future fulfillment of the Feast of Tabernacles is detailed in the following New Testament verses:

And I saw thrones, and they sat on them, and judgment was committed to them. Then I saw the souls of those who had been beheaded for their witness to Jesus and for the word of God, who had not worshiped the beast or his image, and had not received his mark on their foreheads or on their hands. And they lived and reigned with Christ for a thousand years. (Revelation 20:4)

CONCLUSION

Christ fulfilled the spring Feasts of Passover (death), the Feast of Unleavened Bread (burial), and the Feast of Firstfruits (resurrection), and the disciples were imbued with the Holy Spirit on Pentecost exactly fifty days after Passover, exactly fulfilling God's exact divine appointments.

So why go through the trouble of showing Christ fulfilling the spring feasts? I wholeheartedly believe that if He fulfilled the spring feasts, He will fulfill the fall feasts. For if Christ fulfilled the spring feasts and Christ never changes, as He *is* the same yesterday, today, and forever (Hebrews 3:8), then Christ will fulfill the fall feasts. The next feast on God's divine appointment calendar is the Feast of Trumpets, and the next expectation for Christians is the rapture. Could it be that they are both one and the same event? Based on the biblical evidence I have just provided, I believe the answer is yes. As previously listed there are many names for the Feast of Trumpets. I'll discuss in Chapter 3 how these names, themes, and idioms herald the rapture of the bride of Christ on the Feast of Trumpets.

Chapter 2

RAPTURE OF THE CHURCH (BRIDE OF CHRIST)

The word *rapture* does not appear anywhere in the Bible. However, it has its roots in the Bible, in the Greek language. *Rapture* comes from the Greek word *harpazo*, meaning "to seize, catch (away, up), pluck, pull, take (by force)."[9] *Harpazo* was then translated in to the Latin word *raptare*, meaning to "seize and carry off"[10] and *raptor*, meaning "one who seizes by force, robber"[11], which is where the word for the birds of prey with the

---

[9] *Yahweh Restoration Ministry*. (2014, February 5). Retrieved from Bible Study Resources Strong's Concordance with Hebrew and Greek Lexicon searches: http://www.yrm.org/strongs/726

[10] *Merriam-Webster*. (2014, February 5). Retrieved from http://www.merriam-webster.com/dictionary/dual?show=0&t=1391665023

[11] *Dictionary.com*. (2014, 02 08). Retrieved from Copyright © 2014 Dictionary.com, LLC.: http://dictionary.reference.com/browse/raptor

same name came from. Raptors include eagles, falcons, hawks, and vultures that "seize and carry off" their prey. These Latin words were then translated in to the English word that we use today: *rapture*, the act of carrying off.[12]

Many Old Testament verses that support the rapture, such as:

> Now Mount Sinai was completely in smoke, because the Lord descended upon it in fire. Its smoke ascended like the smoke of a furnace, and the whole mountain quaked greatly. And when the blast of the trumpet sounded long and became louder and louder, Moses spoke, and God answered him by voice. Then the Lord came down upon Mount Sinai, on the top of the mountain. And the Lord called Moses to the top of the mountain, and Moses went up. (Exodus 19:18–20)

> Your dead shall live; Together with my dead body they shall arise. Awake and sing, you who dwell in dust; For your dew is like the dew of herbs, and the earth shall cast out the dead. Come, my people, enter your chambers, and

---

[12] *Dictionary.com*. (2014, 02 08). Retrieved from Copyright © 2014 Dictionary.com, LLC.: http://dictionary.reference.com/browse/rapture

shut your doors behind you; Hide yourself, as it were, for a little moment, Until the indignation is past. For behold, the Lord comes out of His place to punish the inhabitants of the earth for their iniquity; The earth will also disclose her blood, And will no more cover her slain. (Isaiah 26:19–21)

There are many New Testament verses that also support the rapture, such as:

But of that day and hour no one knows, not even the angels of heaven, but My Father   only. (Matthew 24:36)

Then the kingdom of heaven shall be likened to ten virgins who took their lamps and went out to meet the Bridegroom. Now five of them were wise, and five were foolish. Those who were foolish took their lamps and took no oil with them, but   the wise took oil in their vessels with their lamps. But while the Bridegroom was delayed, they all slumbered and slept. And at midnight a cry was heard: "Behold, the Bridegroom is coming; go out to meet him!" Then all those virgins arose and trimmed their lamps. And the foolish said to the wise, "Give us some of your oil, for our lamps are going out." But the wise answered, saying, "No, lest there should not be enough for us and you; but go rather to those who sell, and buy for yourselves." And while they went to buy, the Bridegroom came, and those who were ready went in with him to the wedding; and the door was shut. Afterward the other virgins came also, saying, "Lord, Lord, open to us!" But he answered and said, "Assuredly, I say to you, I do not know you." Watch therefore, for you know neither the day nor the hour in which the Son of Man is coming. (Matthew 25:1-13)

Jesus said to her, "I am the resurrection and the life. He who believes in Me, though he may die, he shall live. And whoever lives and believes in Me shall never die." (John11:25-26)

Now this I say, brethren, that flesh and blood cannot inherit the kingdom of God; nor does corruption inherit incorruption. Behold, I tell you a mystery: We shall not all sleep, but we shall all be changed—in a moment, in the twinkling of an eye, at the last trumpet. For the trumpet will sound, and the dead will be raised incorruptible, and we shall be changed. (1 Corinthians 15:50-52)

For this we say to you by the word of the Lord, that we who are alive and remain until the coming of the Lord will by no means precede those who are asleep. For the Lord Himself will descend from heaven with a shout, with the voice of an archangel, and with the trumpet of God. And the dead in Christ will rise first. Then we who are alive and remain shall be caught up together with them in the clouds to meet the Lord in the air. And thus we shall always be with the Lord. Therefore comfort one another with these words. (1 Thessalonians 4:15–18)

For the mystery of lawlessness is already at work; only He who now restrains will do so until He is taken out of the way. And then the lawless one will be revealed, whom the Lord will consume with the breath of His mouth and destroy with the brightness of His coming. (2 Thessalonians 2:7–8)

After these things I looked, and behold, a door standing open in heaven. And the first voice which I heard was like a trumpet speaking with me, saying, "Come up here, and I will show you things which must take place after this." Immediately I was in the Spirit; and behold, a throne set in heaven, and One sat on the throne. (Revelation 4:1–2)

Chapter 3

TYING THE TWO TOGETHER (FEAST OF TRUMPETS AND THE RAPTURE)

The names, themes, and idioms of the Feast of Trumpets as listed in Chapter 1 speak to the rapture occurring on the Feast of Trumpets. The first name on the list is The Day of the Awakening Blast.[13] In the Old Testament, the Feast of Trumpets is also known in Hebrew as *Yom Teruah* (pronounced: ter-oo-aw'), meaning "an awakening blast, clamor, i.e. acclamation of joy or a battle-cry; especially clangor of trumpets, as an alarm: alarm, blow(- ing) (of, the) (trumpets), joy, jubilee, loud noise, rejoicing, a shout(-ing), (high, joyful) sound(-ing).[14] With regard to Yom

---

[13] Chumney, E. (2014, 02 8). *Friends of Sabbath*. Retrieved from Friends of Sabbath: http://www.friendsofsabbath.org/Further_Research/ Holy%20Days/The-Seven-Festivals-of-the-Messiah.pdf/Page 105

[14] *Yahweh Restoration Ministry*. (2014, February 5). Retrieved from Bible Study Resources Strong's Concordance with Hebrew and Greek Lexicon searches: http://www.yrm.org/strongs/8643

Teruah, the image most used in the Bible to describe the Feast of Trumpets are an awakening blast (of trumpet) bringing our souls to repentance and shouting.

FEAST OF TRUMPETS:
THE AWAKENING BLAST/SHOUT

So how do these names used to describe the Feast of Trumpets relate to the rapture of the church? Before getting into this, I wanted to first discuss what the bride's responsibility is to Christ, the Bridegroom. Christians are called to be spiritually awake, ever ready and watching for the Bridegroom's return. Those who are prepared will take part in Christ's return during the rapture, which is heralded by an awakening (trumpet) blast and a shout. This is illustrated in the parable of the ten virgins (Matthew 25:1-13).

In this parable the Bridegroom is delayed and suddenly a cry or shout is heard announcing His arrival. Though all ten virgins had been physically sleeping, the five who were spiritually awake and watching to the possibility of the Bridegroom's return had enough oil—representing the Holy Spirit—(Luke 4:18; Acts 10:38)—in their lamps. They quickly trimmed the wicks, lit their way to the wedding procession, and were ushered in to the Bridegroom's wedding party. However, the five virgins who were spiritually unprepared were caught by surprise by the midnight cry, having little oil in their lamps. They went to buy oil for their lamps after the other five virgins would not give them any oil as they would not have enough for themselves. As a result, the virgins who were unprepared were late to the wedding celebration and were denied entry to the Bridegroom's wedding by Jesus saying, "I do not know you."

Were these five unprepared virgins Christians or nonbelievers? I believe they were believers that was treated by Christ as unbelievers as they were oblivious to God's divine appointment.

Why did Christ use the number ten instead of six or seven or any other number for the number of virgins? I believe He used a factor of ten, and in this case, ten to the first power, as ten is representative of the total of 100 percent. Therefore, this parable is saying in the simplest of terms that 50 percent of the church will make it to heaven via the rapture and 50 percent will be rebuked by Christ. This 50 percent will go through the tribulation period and will most likely be beheaded along with others who come to know Christ during this period (Revelation 20:4).

Christ will be as a thief in the night unto us, and why should we expect anything less? A bride is always prepared and ready for the Bridegroom. A bride is always watching even if physically asleep. The bride always anticipates that the Bridegroom could come at any moment. This interpretation of the parable is further supported by Christ's parable of the faithful servant and evil servant wherein He says He will come on a day and hour that the servant is not expecting and will cut this evil servant in two and appoint this evil servant's portion with unbelievers (Luke 12:46).

This reading of these two parables is also supported by many additional New Testament verses that warn Christians to be spiritually awake and watching for Christ's return (bolding is for emphasis):

> But know this, that if the master of the house had known what hour the thief would come, he would have **watched** and not allowed his house to be broken into. (Matthew 24:43)

> **Watch** therefore, and pray always that you may be counted worthy to escape all these things that will come to pass, and to stand before the Son of Man. (Luke 21:36)

> Assuredly, I say to you, this generation will by no means pass away till all these things take place. Heaven and earth will pass away, but My words will by no means pass away. No One Knows the Day or Hour "But of that day and hour no one knows, not even the angels in heaven, nor the Son, but only the Father. Take heed, watch and pray; for you do not know when the time is. It is like a man going to a far country, who left his

house and gave authority to his servants, and to each his work, and commanded the doorkeeper to watch. **Watch** therefore, for you do not know when the master of the house is coming—in the evening, at midnight, at the crowing of the rooster, or in the morning— lest, coming suddenly, he find you sleeping. (Mark 13:30–36)

But concerning the times and the seasons, brethren, you have no need that I should write to you. For you yourselves know perfectly that the day of the Lord so comes as a thief in the night. For when they say, "Peace and safety!" then sudden destruction comes upon them, as labor pains upon a pregnant woman. And they shall not escape. But you, brethren, are not in darkness, so that this Day should overtake you as a thief. You are all sons of light and sons of the day. We are not of the night nor of darkness. Therefore let us not sleep, as others do, but let us **watch** and be sober. (1 Thessalonians 5:1–6)

Remember therefore how you have received and heard; hold fast and repent. Therefore if you will not **watch**, I will come upon you as a thief, and you will not know what hour I will come upon you. (Revelation 3:3)

In several verses in the Old and New Testaments, the

rapture is preceded by a shout, the blast of a trumpet, or both for those Christians who are spiritually prepared, ready, awake, and watching for Christ's return.

An example of the rapture occurs in the Old Testament when Moses and the Israelites were in the wilderness and camped at the foot of Mount Sinai.

> Now Mount Sinai was completely in smoke, because the Lord descended upon it in fire. Its smoke ascended like the smoke of a furnace, and the whole mountain quaked greatly. And when the blast of the trumpet sounded long and became louder and louder, Moses spoke, and God answered him by voice. Then the Lord came down upon Mount Sinai, on the top of the mountain. And the Lord called Moses to the top of the mountain and Moses went up. (Exodus 19:18–20)

In this verse, Mount Sinai was covered in smoke (representing clouds) as God descended. Then a blast of a trumpet sounded long and grew louder and louder. God then calls Moses up on to Mount Sinai with His voice (representative of shout), and Moses goes up. This Old Testament depiction is a picture of the rapture, mirroring the New Testament picture of the rapture. The New Testament says that Jesus will descend from heaven with a shout and with the trumpet of God, and the dead and the living in Christ will be caught up to meet Him in the clouds in the air. (1 Thessalonians 4:16–17)

Another verse in the New Testament where the rapture is heralded by a trumpet ca be found in Revelation 4:1–3, wherein John hears a voice speaking like a trumpet telling him to "come up here," and when John obeys he is immediately in the spirit. This is a picture of the rapture for many reasons. First, John (representing the bride of Christ) is immediately in heaven after God calls him. Second, the scripture does not mention the church until Revelation 19 when Christ returns with His bride. This suggests that God will deal with Israel without the church being present.

In another New Testament verse, the rapture is heralded by a trumpet and/or a shout:

Now this I say, brethren, that flesh and blood cannot inherit the kingdom of God; nor does corruption inherit incorruption. Behold, I tell you a mystery: We shall not all sleep, but we shall all be changed—in a moment, in the twinkling of an eye, at the last trumpet. For the trumpet will sound, and the dead will be raised incorruptible, and we shall be changed. (1 Corinthians 15:50–52).

FEAST OF TRUMPETS:
THE WEDDING CEREMONY

The Feast of Trumpets is also called the Wedding Ceremony. Collectively, Christians are called the bride of Christ (Ephesians 5:25–32; Revelation 19:7–9). The Bridegroom is now preparing a home for His bride in heaven and will return in the clouds, rapturing His bride unto Himself (John 14:2–3).

The wedding ceremony as provided by God to the Jewish people is a picture of the redemption of humanity, culminating in the marriage supper of the lamb. With this in mind, a quick synopsis of the Jewish wedding ceremony consists of twelve steps:[15]

1. The selection of the bride (via the Holy Spirit [John16:7–8]).

2. Establishing the price for the bride (Death of Christ on the Cross [1 Peter 1:18–19]) with bride and groom now betrothed as part of the first two steps of the marriage process, legally binding bride and groom in a marriage contract, though

---

[15] Chumney, E. (2014, 02 8). *Friends of Sabbath*. Retrieved from Friends of Sabbath: http://www.friendsofsabbath.org/Further_Research/ Holy%20Days/The-Seven-Festivals-of-the-Messiah.pdf/Page 121

they do not live together[16]. (Giving your life to Christ (John 3:16)),

3. The bride and groom are betrothed to each other.

4. A written document called a betrothal contract is drawn (all the promises of God are written in the Bible [2 Corinthians 1:20]).

5. The bride must give consent (giving your life to Christ [Romans 10:8–10]).

6. Gifts are given to the bride by the groom (the gift being the Holy Spirit [John 14:26]).

7. The bride is immersed in water, indicating a separation from the previous life outside of Christ (baptized in Christ [Romans 6:4]).

8. The Bridegroom departs to his father's house to prepare a home for himself and the bride (ascension of Jesus [John 14:1–3]).

9. The bride is consecrated and set apart for a period of time while the Bridegroom is away building the house (bride is separated from the world [consecrated], while watching and waiting for the Bridegroom [Romans 6:1–4]).

10. The Bridegroom returns with a shout and blowing of trumpet or horn, known as a *shofar* (a

---

[16] Chumney, E. (2014, 02 8). *Friends of Sabbath*. Retrieved from Friends of Sabbath: http://www.friendsofsabbath.org/Further_Research/Holy%20Days/The-Seven-Festivals-of-the-Messiah.pdf/Page 123

shout and blasting of a trumpet prior to rapture is mentioned in Matthew 25:6; 1 Thessalonians 4:16–17; Revelation 4:1]).

11. The Bridegroom abducts bride (rapture [1 Corinthians 15:52]).

12. Finally, a marriage supper is held (marriage supper of the Lamb [Revelation 19:9]).

I wanted to further discuss the Bridegroom abducting the bride of Christ alongside Christ rapturing His bride or the bride being carried off or lifted up to meet the Bridegroom. Today, Jewish marriages are conducted under a *Hupah* or canopy. However, this was not always the case. Today, the *Hupah* is representative of the litter on which the bride was carried aloft, being lifted up with wooden poles and then carried to the groom.[17] The poles were made from branches of trees planted in the years when the bride and groom were born.[18]

While, the entire Jewish marriage ceremony speaks of Christ's marriage to His bride, the litter that gave rise to the *Hupah* and the practice of lifting the bride and carrying her to the bridegroom is symbolic of the bride of Christ being raptured or lifted up to Him through Christ's death, burial, resurrection, and a Christian's

---

[17] Edidin, B. M. (1941). *Jewish Customs and Ceremonies*. New York: Hebrew Publishing Company.

[18] Edidin, B. M. (1941). *Jewish Customs and Ceremonies*. New York: Hebrew Publishing Company.

realization through the prompting of the Holy Spirit that we need to be born again at the foot of the cross. The branch(es) of the Christian's *Hupa* is the wooden cross that uplifts us to Christ when we were born again and ultimately to Christ in the air during the rapture.

FEAST OF TRUMPETS: RESURRECTION OF THE DEAD

The Feast of Trumpets is also known as the Resurrection of the Dead. Notably the thirteenth principle of the Jewish faith is the resurrectionof the dead[19], and in accordance with the Talmud, the dead will be resurrected on the Feast of Trumpets.[20] When the rapture occurs, the dead in Christ will arise first to be gathered together with the rest of the bride who is alive in the air to be with Christ forever more (1 Corinthians 15:52; 1 Thessalonians 413–18; Isaiah 26:19).

---

[19] Chumney, E. (2014, 02 8). *Friends of Sabbath*. Retrieved from Friends of Sabbath: http://www.friendsofsabbath.org/Further_Research/ Holy%20Days/The-Seven-Festivals-of-the-Messiah.pdf/Page 132

[20] Chumney, E. (2014, 02 8). *Friends of Sabbath*. Retrieved from Friends of Sabbath: http://www.friendsofsabbath.org/Further_Research/ Holy%20Days/The-Seven-Festivals-of-the-Messiah.pdf/Page 132

FEAST OF TRUMPETS:
THE LAST TRUMP

The Feast of Trumpets is so named because a lot of trumpets or *shofars* are blown during this feast. In the Old Testament, this feast is described in the following way:

> Then the Lord spoke to Moses, saying, "Speak to the children of Israel, saying: 'In the seventh month, on the first day of the month, you shall have a sabbath-rest, a memorial of blowing of trumpets, a holy convocation. You shall do no customary work on it; and you shall offer an offering made by fire to the Lord.'" (Leviticus 23:23–25)

During this feast, the *shofar* is blown 100 times[21]. These blasts consist of *Tekiah*, a single, medium-length blast that transitions from low to high pitch and has a hard, short push on the low pitch, a slight sustain on the high pitch, and sometimes ends with a short, higher-pitch burst; *Shevarim*, three blasts of low to high, rather like three short *Tekiah* without the short burst on the ends; and *Teruah*, rapid single-second, staccato bursts of which there should be nine or more. The last

---

[21] http://www.chabad.org/holidays/JewishNewYear/template_cdo/aid/4837/jewish/Shofar.htm

trump is the *Tekiah Gedolah*, similar to Tekiah, only with the high note sustained for the longest possible breath and ended with a violent, short breath of an even higher-pitched note.[22] In other words, the *Tekiah Gedolah* or Great Blast[23] is the loudest of all four and is held the longest, growing louder at the end. This was the trumpet sound that led Moses up Mount Sinai (Exodus 19:18–20).

Just as God's Tekiah Gedola and not one made by humans drew Moses up Mount Sinai, the trumpet blast hearlding the rapture will be God's Last Trump during the Feast of Trumpets. I also believe that God's perspective on a new moon may be slightly different than humanity's as God's vantage point is different. We can not see the new moon until it transitions far enough away from the sun to be visible. God does not have that limitation, and He will decide exactly when the new moon begins and when Feast of Trumpets starts/ends (on the day He decides, it will start around twilight). Additionally, when Paul wrote the letter to the church at Corinth, stating "that in a moment, in the twinkling of an eye, at the last trumpet ... the trumpet will sound, and the dead will be raised incorruptible,

---

[22] Bingamon, D. (2014, 03 18). *The Shofar Users Manual.* Retrieved from BIBLICAL INSTRUMENT SERIES A Guide for Shofar Players: http://www.bingamon.com/jubilee/shofar.htm

[23] Project, A. C. (1971). *Encyclopaedia Judaica Vol 14.* Jerusalem: Keter Publishing House Ltd.

and we shall be changed" (1 Corinthians 15:52), we don't have a letter back to Paul asking for more details. This silence is deafening. The Christian church at the time when Paul wrote the letter was comprised of believing Jews who practiced the Lord's feast days, and this was a part of their heritage, customs, and practices. They understood what Paul was talking about—the Feast of Trumpets. If the church members had any doubt as to Paul's meaning in this letter, they would have asked. If they wanted to know anything, it was when their Lord would return. But they understood what Paul was saying, so they did nto ask Paul for any clarifying remarks, as these would have appeared in the second letter to the Corinthians. And, of course, the church members did not ask for clarification about what the last trump meant.

FEAST OF TRUMPETS:
THE HIDDEN DAY OR DAY OF CONCEALMENT

The Feast of Trumpets is also known as The Hidden Day or Day of Concealment. After Christ's bride is raptured, the bride will be hidden in the wedding chamber until the seven-year tribulation is over. This is clearly shown in the following Old Testament verses:

Come, my people, enter your chambers, and shut your doors behind you; Hide yourself, as it were, for a little moment, until the indignation is past. For behold, the Lord comes out of His place to punish the inhabitants of the earth for their iniquity; the earth will also disclose her blood, and will no more cover her slain. (Isaiah 26:20-21)

Seek the Lord, all you meek of the earth, who have upheld His justice. Seek righteousness, seek humility. It may be that you will be hidden In the day of the Lord's anger. (Zephaniah 2:3)

For in the time of trouble He shall hide me in His pavilion; in the secret place of His tabernacle He shall hide me; He shall set me high upon a rock. (Psalm 27:5)

The Hidden Day also references the Feast of Trumpets, which no one knows the day or hour of(Psalm 81:3). This is because the Feast of Trumpets will occur on the new moon, validated by two witnesses, and no one knows the day or hour when this moon will be spotted.

Additionally, Christ spoke of His return being on a day that no one knows the time of, not even the angels, but only His Father. As His Jewish deciples understood the Feast of Trumpets to be the hidden day, they knew that what Christ said was an idiom for this feast. This is proven by the fact that the Feast of Trumpets is the only day in the entire year that was referred to as the hidden day or the day that no man knew the day or hou Jewish customs and practice. So this statement validates rather than excludes the Feast of Trumpets, especially if one keeps it in context with the other Jewish meanings for this feast.

Feast of Trumpets: Time of Jacob's Trouble or Birth Pangs of the Messiah

The Time of Jacob's Trouble is another name for the Birth Pangs of the Messiah and speaks to the seven-year tribulation period, which begins a short time after the rapture. In this context, Jacob is Israel, indicating that the Nation of Israel will be tremendously tested such that two-thirds of its people will die during the this time. Zechariah prophesied:

> "And it shall come to pass in all the land," says the Lord, "That two-thirds in it shall be cut off and die, But one-third shall be left in it: I will bring the one-third through the fire, will refine them as silver is refined, And test them as gold is tested. They will call on My name, And I will

answer them. I will say, 'This is My people'; And each one will say, 'The Lord is my God.'" (Zechariah 13:8–9)

Other verses describing the Time of Jacob's Trouble in the Old and New Testaments are:

Now these are the words that the Lord spoke concerning Israel and Judah. For thus says the Lord: We have heard a voice of trembling, of fear, and not of peace. Ask now, and see, whether a man is ever in labor with child? So why do I see every man with his hands on his loins like a woman in labor, and all faces turned pale? Alas! For that day is great, so that none is like it; and it is the time of Jacob's trouble, but he shall be saved out of it. (Jeremiah 30:4–7)

A woman, when she is in labor, has sorrow because her hour has come; but as soon as she has given birth to the child, she no longer remembers the anguish, for joy that a human being has been born into the world. Therefore you now have sorrow; but I will see you again and your heart will rejoice, and your joy no one will take from you. (John 16:21–22)

But concerning the times and the seasons, brethren, you have no need that I should write to you. For you yourselves know perfectly that the day of the Lord so comes as a thief in the night. For when they say, "Peace and safety!" then sudden destruction comes upon them, as labor pains upon a pregnant woman. And they shall not escape. (1Thessalonians 5:1-3)

Chapter 4

TWINKLING OF AN EYE

In studying the Bible throughout my life I have been deeply intrigued with the verse, "In a moment, in the twinkling of an eye, at the last trumpet. For the trumpet will sound, and the dead will be raised incorruptible, and we shall be changed" (1 Corinthians 15:52). What does "blinking of an eye" mean? I thought, and still do, that it means the rapture will happen so fast it will only be noticeable because of the number of people who are gone. A twinkle or blink of an eye is 3/10 to 4/10 of a second or 300 to 400 milliseconds.[24]

However, I believe "twinkling of an eye" has a deeper meaning other than how fast an eye blinks. To understand it, we must again look to Jewish customs, tradition, and practice.

---

[24] *Medicine* (2014, February 19). http://www.madsci.org/posts/archives/1998-11/911697403.Me.r.html

In Judaism, the term "twinkling of an eye" taught that "as to twilight, it is doubtful whether it is part day or part night, or whether all of it is day or all of it is night ... Twilight is like the twinkling of an eye as the night enters and the day departs, and it is impossible to determine its length."[25] This view is further reinforced by the following depiction of the Jewish day.[26]

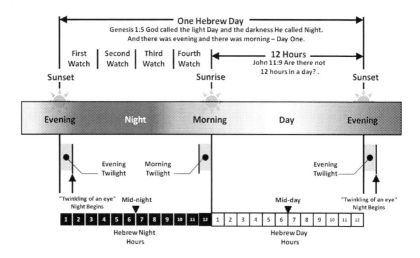

A biblical or Jewish twenty-four-hour day begins at sunset and transitions through evening twilight to night, to morning twilight to day, to sunset.[27] The first

[25] Dotlich, R. K. (2008). *Righteous Indignation: A Jewish Call For Justice.* Woodstock: Jewish Lights Publishing.

[26] *TorahCalendar.com* (2014, February 19). http://www.torahcalendar.com/SUNSET.asp

[27] *TorahCalendar.com* (2014, February 19). http://www.torahcalendar.com/SUNSET.asp

half or twelve hours of a Hebrew day lasts from the beginning of sunset to the beginning of sunrise and is divided into four three-hour periods called watches (Matthew 14:28; Luke 12:38). The second half of a Hebrew day lasts from a moment of sunrise to moment of sunset, wherein sunrise is defined as to the time at which the sun's upper edge begins to appear above the earth's horizon in the east.[28]

Hebraic thought understands evening twilight to be a transitional period between day and night.[29] It is defined and understood by Jewish custom and practice as occurring at a specific moment when two medium-size stars can be seen with the naked eye, and that twilight becomes night when a third medium-size star appears.[30] In biblical times, Hebraic customs, practice, and tradition understood night to begin at the moment known as the twinkling of an eye.[31] This is very interesting from a prophetic point of view, as Paul also

---

[28] *TorahCalendar.com* (2014, February 19). http://www.torahcalendar.com/SUNSET.asp

[29] *TorahCalendar.com* (2014, February 19). http://www.torahcalendar.com/SUNSET.asp

[30] *TorahCalendar.com* (2014, February 19). http://www.torahcalendar.com/SUNSET.asp

[31] *TorahCalendar.com* (2014, February 19). http://www.torahcalendar.com/SUNSET.asp

prophesied that the righteous would be resurrected in the twinkling of an eye.[32]

So the phrase "twinkling of an eye" can have dual meanings that are both accurate and occurring simultaneously. One meaning is that it happens very quickly, and the other is twilight when the night enters and the day departs. The two definitions of the twinkling of an eye can occur simultaneously. For example, such as the rapture occurring in the twinkling of an eye (in 300 to 400 milliseconds) and during the twinkling of an eye (at the moment when night begins). Finally, the *shofar* must only be blown during the day[33] with evening twilight being the last opportunity to sound the last trump, the *Tekiah Gedolah*, before nightfall.

---

[32] *TorahCalendar.com* (2014, February 19). http://www.torahcalendar.com/SUNSET.asp

[33] Project, A. C. (1971). *Encyclopaedia Judaica Vol 14*. Jerusalem: Keter Publishing House Ltd

Chapter 5

FOUR BLOOD MOONS
AND SOLAR ECLIPSE

W hat is a blood moon? It is a lunar eclipse wherein sunlight passes through the earth's atmosphere, bending the light around the edges of the planet and thereby causing the shadow of the earth to appear red with regard to the reflection of the moon back to the earth.[34] A *tetrad* is four eclipses in a short period of time. Four successive blood moons are not very common, with only three such events occurring in the last 500 years (see chart).

What is the significance of a blood moon and a solar eclipse? A blood moon represents a warning to the

---

[34] Faulkner Dr., D. R. (2013, 07 12). *Answersingenesis.org*. Retrieved from Will Lunar Eclipses Cause Four Blood Moons in 2014 and 2015: http://www.answersingenesis.org/articles/2013/07/12/lunar-eclipses-cause-blood-moons

nation of Israel, and a solar eclipse serves as a warning to the nations of the world.[35]

Pastor Hagee and Mark Biltz have been talking about the four blood moons a lot in their sermons lately, and rightly so. The last three blood moon tetrads that occurred in 1492 and 1493, 1949 and 1950, and 1967 and 1968 trumpeted Israel finding a new homeland, respectively the Spanish Diaspora via Edict of Expulsion, Israel being reborn in a day, and Israel regaining total control over Jerusalem.

Granted, the three previous blood moon tetrads occurred after these specific events; however, one cannot deny that these three historical blood moon tetrads occurred on Passover and Tabernacles and that each sought to mark in the heavens a momentous event that preceded it. I agree with Pastor Hagee in his three-part sermon on the four blood moons that for each tetrad there were tears followed by victory for the Jewish people. For example, in 1492 and 1493, the Jews were banished from Spain by Queen Isabella and King Ferdinand's Edict of Expulsion, leading to many Jews financing Columbus' voyages that ultimately led to the discovery the New World and a home away from home for the Jewish people where they could prosper. The four blood moons trumpeted this victory for the

---

[35] Unknown last name, M. (2014, 02 23). *The Fig Tree Generation.* Retrieved from The Coming FOUR Blood Moons: http://figtree-generation.blogspot.com/p/the.html

Jewish People. Interestingly, after the Spanish Edict of Expulsion, resulting in the Jewish Diaspora from Spain, Spain's economic prowess was doomed. Even today 522 years later Spain has asked the Diaspora Jews' descendants to return as the country recognizes how hardworking and how blessed the work of their Jewish hands would be in today's economy.[36]

Before 1948 and 1949, six million Jews died during the Nazi holocaust. Despite that devastating event in Jewish history—and for humankind, for that matter—on May 14, 1948, Israel was reborn in a single day, marking a victory for the Jewish people and fulfilling Bible prophecy at the same time as detailed by the following prophetic verses written thousands of years ago:

> "The hand of the Lord came upon me and brought me out in the Spirit of the Lord, and set me down in the midst of the valley; and it was full of bones. Then He caused me to pass by them all around, and behold, there were very many in the open valley; and indeed they were very dry. And He said to me, "Son of man, can these bones live?" So I answered, "O Lord God, You know." Again He said to me, "Prophesy to these bones, and say to them, 'O dry bones, hear

[36] Hadden, G. (2013, 03 06). *BBC News Magazine*. Retrieved from Sephardic Jews invited back to Spain after 500 years: http://www.bbc.com/news/magazine-21631427

the word of the Lord!'" Thus says the Lord God
to these bones: "Surely I will cause breath to
enter into you, and you shall live ... these bones
are the whole house of Israel." (Ezekiel 37:1–14)

"Before she was in labor, she gave birth; Before
her pain came, she delivered a male child. Who
has heard such a thing? Who has seen such
things? Shall the earth be made to give birth in
one day?" (Isaiah 66:7–8)

The four blood moons trumpeted this victory of Israel
being born in a day in 1949 and 1950.

In 1967, Israel was attacked on all sides by those who
would drive her into the sea to the point that Moshe
Dayan, the Israeli Defense Minister, had briefed Prime
Minister Golda Meir of the Samson option[37] (Use of
nuclear weapons by Israel) as a possible reality, as
Israel had thought all had been lost because the Arab
invasion was so overwhelming. However, Israel turned
the tide in battle and won such a great victory that
the Soviets threatened to become involved in the war.
Israel also took control of East Jerusalem from Jordan
during the Six-Day War with Israel now in total control
of Jerusalem (West Jerusalem was taken in 1948 when

[37] Lindsay, H. (2007, 07 14). *WND Commentary*. Retrieved from The
Samson Option: http://www.wnd.com/2007/07/42560/

Israel became a nation).[38] The four blood moons in 1967 and 1968 trumpeted this victory of Israel.

Historical Four Blood Moon (Tetrad) Patterns

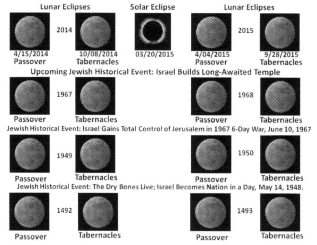

Lunar Eclipses		Solar Eclipse	Lunar Eclipses	
2014			2015	
4/15/2014 Passover	10/08/2014 Tabernacles	03/20/2015 Passover	4/04/2015 Passover	9/28/2015 Tabernacles

Upcoming Jewish Historical Event: Israel Builds Long-Awaited Temple

1967			1968	
Passover	Tabernacles		Passover	Tabernacles

Jewish Historical Event: Israel Gains Total Control of Jerusalem in 1967 6-Day War, June 10, 1967

1949			1950	
Passover	Tabernacles		Passover	Tabernacles

Jewish Historical Event: The Dry Bones Live; Israel Becomes Nation in a Day, May 14, 1948.

1492			1493	
Passover	Tabernacles		Passover	Tabernacles

Jewish Historical Event: Spain's Edict of Expulsion in 1492; Christopher Columbus Sails Partially Financed by the Jewish People

The next blood moon tetrad will take place in 2014 and 2015, and sandwiched between the two blood moons in 2014 and the two blood moons 2015 will be a full solar eclipse.[39] After taking all prophetic signposts in the heavens in to account with regard to Jewish feasts, the blood moon tetrad, and the great sign, that the four blood moons of 2014 and 2015 will not come after any specific event as they did before. They will now come

---

[38] *Wikipedia the Free Encyclopedia.* (2014, 02 23). Retrieved from Jerusalem: http://en.wikipedia.org/wiki/Jerusalem

[39] Unknown. (2014, 02 23). *NASA Eclipse Website.* Retrieved from Lunar Eclipse Page: http://eclipse.gsfc.nasa.gov/lunar.html

before specific world-shaking events, including the rapture of the bride of Christ, the Antichrist signing the seven-year covenant with Israel, and the dragon being thrown down to the earth and chasing the woman who flees into the wilderness. (In Chapter 8 I'll put all these pieces together.) This belief is further supported by the fact that there has not been an earth-shattering event from Israel's perspective that the four blood moons would be heralding. If there has been such an event, I am unaware of it.

Additionally, as the time grows ever closer to the rapture of the bride by the Bridegroom, God's focus on the nation of Israel continues to reduce down to a rich end-times event, the Antichrist's signing of the seven-year covenant with Israel and Israel's subsequent building of Israel's third temple. The second blood moon tetrad in 1949 and 1950 heralded Israel's rebirth as a nation. The third blood moon tetrad in 1967 and 1968 heralded Israel's total control over Jerusalem. The fourth blood moon in 2014 and 2015 will herald Israel's rebuilding of their long-awaited third temple.

Chapter 6

BOOK OF REVELATION— KEEPING IT SIMPLE

Throughout the ages, the book of Revelation has been very mysterious. Part of the reason is that God has hidden many things in this book, not to mention the Bible in general, that are sealed until the end times (Daniel 12:4).

The book of Revelation is chronological. The first three chapters detail the seven churches or church age, followed by John (representative of the church) being raptured to heaven (Revelation 4:1). After John is raptured, there is a slight lapse in time whereby John writes what he is seeing in heaven from an administrative point of view. Then John writes about Christ who is able to open the first seal, completing Chapter 5. Then in Chapters 6 through 11, John begins to document what he sees of the tribulation period, seals being broken, trumpets being blown, the two witnesses' deaths and resurrections, and the seventh trumpet being blown. Beginning in Chapter 12, John tells us about a great sign in heaven of a woman clothed in the sun with a crown of twelve stars above her head and the moon at her feet, and then being with child she cried out in pain. This great sign is followed by another sign where a great fiery, red dragon having seven heads and ten horns was thrown out of heaven to earth with the dragon drawing with its tail a third of the angels with him. The dragon then persecutes the woman, who flees into the wilderness to a place prepared by God. This marks the end of the first half of the tribulation period as 1,260 days are left. The second half of the tribulation is marked by bowl judgments and the second coming of Christ on a white horse along with His bride who was raptured in Revelation 4:1. Satan is then bound, and the 1,000-year millennial reign begins. After the 1,000 years, Satan is loosed and then defeated by Christ, followed by the great white throne judgment and a new heaven and a new earth.

It is critical to recognize that the book of Revelation is chronological. Because of this, the timeline of the end times can be established and relied upon as long as one keeps it in context with the totality of the Scriptures.

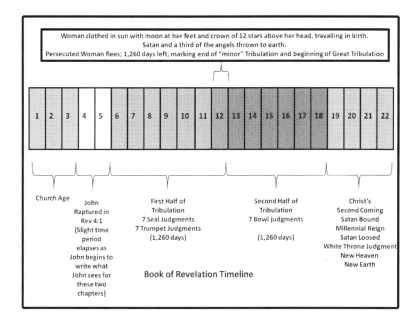

The three things I want to discuss with regard
to specific events that John saw are in Revelation 12.
Specifically, the great sign in heaven of a woman
clothed in the sun with a crown of twelve stars above
her head and the moon at her feet, travailing in pain as
she gives birth; the great fiery red dragon with seven
heads and ten horns drawing with its tail a third of
the angels with him as he falls from heaven; and the
dragon's persecution of the woman, who flees into the
wilderness to a place prepared by God. So let's take
a journey together, looking at these three events that
John saw.

Chapter 7

THE GREAT SIGN
SATAN THROWN TO EARTH
WOMAN FLEES IN TO
THE WILDERNESS

God set the stars in the heavens for divine appointments and for signs (Genesis 1:14). Therefore, we have an obligation to search out what God has hidden in the stars (Proverbs 25:2). In this case, God made it simpler because He gave clues to John that can help us. This makes sense, I believe, as there is so much at stake regarding our eternal souls that God wants us to not have any excuse for not being spiritually prepared, ready, awake, and watching. Not that we would have any excuse in any way, as the heavens and all of creation declare God the Creator (Psalm 19:1). However, this is just another clue that God provides to help seal the deal for those who are interested in Him and searching Him out.

Truly, the great sign is a significant event, otherwise God wouldn't have shown it to John. Of all things God could have shown John, why did He show him this great sign? There has to be a purpose. Again, I believe God is providing us with one more clue to when the prophetic events would occur. Additionally, nowhere in the entire Bible is there another great sign in heaven that we are to be looking for from a prophetic standpoint (a signpost). The great sign John saw was a woman clothed in the sun with the moon at her feet and a crown of twelve stars above her head, travailing in pain as she gives birth. Again, why did God let John see the sign? What is great about this sign? And what are the implications of this great sign for us today?

I believe God showed John the great sign so John could relay the sign to us as. It is a sign for our times as we continue to look forward in unlocking the mysteries of the book of Revelation. Also, without God revealing this sign to us, we would never see it. We would never know it was there because the great sign occurs during the day in Israel, looking toward the eastern sky. So without God's assistance in revealing the sign to John, Israel would never see it. Therefore, God is intentionally revealing His handiwork to us and calling our attention to it.

The great sign can only be seen with planetarium software such as Stellarium, a freeware planetarium software program that shows exactly what you see when you look up at the stars at any point in time and from any location on earth. It can be downloaded at http://www.stellarium.org/.

Once you have Stellarium downloaded on your computer, open the program and move your cursor to the lower left side of your computer screen. This will cause a toolbar to appear. Click on the top icon that looks like a starburst. This will result in a location box appearing. Enter the following information in the location box: name city—Jerusalem, Israel (as all signs in Revelation are seen from Israel), altitude—18M, country—Israel, and planet—Earth. If the latitude and longitude do not automatically load after selecting Jerusalem, Israel, from the drop-down menu, input N 32^0 degrees 0' 0.00 for latitude and E 35^0 degrees 0' 0.00 for longitude. Once all of the information is in the location box, close it. Next click on the clock just below the starburst. A date and time box will appear. Move the date and time box to the upper right of your computer screen to get it out of the way. Next, move your cursor to the bottom left of your computer screen. This will reveal another tool bar. Ensure the following icons are turned on: constellation lines, constellation names, constellation art, cardinal points, ground, atmosphere, and planet names. Ensure the following icons are turned off: equatorial grid, azimuthal grid, and nebulas. Next move the scene on your computer screen with you cursor so the Cardinal Point E (east) is centered at the bottom of the screen. You are now looking east from Jerusalem. Next in the date and time box, ensure date and time reads: 2017 (year) 09 (month) 23 (day) 0 (hour) 0 (minutes) 0 (seconds). Now turn the atmosphere and ground off via the tool bar at bottom left as previously mentioned. Now minimize the picture on the screen with your mouse so that you can see Virgo from her feet to the top of Leo above her head.

So what is it you see? You see a woman (the constellation of Virgo) who is clothed in the sun with the moon at her feet and a garland or crown of twelve stars above her head. The twelve stars consist of the nine that make up the constellation of Leo, plus three wandering stars or planets[40]: Mercury, Venus, and Mars. Additionally, between Virgo's legs is the planet Jupiter, as if the woman is travailing in pain, giving birth.

The constellation of Virgo represents the Virgin Mary (Genesis 3:15; Isaiah 7:14). The constellation of Leo represents the Lion of the Tribe of Judah[41], or, according to Revelation 5:5, Christ. The brightest star in the constellation of Leo is Regulus[42], which is where we get the word *regal*[43]. Jupiter is being birthed between

[40] *Wandering Star* (2014, February 19). http://en.wikipedia.org/wiki/Wandering_star

[41] *Constellations of Words*. (2014, February 19). Retrieved from http://www.constellationsofwords.com/Constellations/Leo.html

[42] *Is There A Gospel in the Stars* (2014, February 19). Retrieved from http://www.setterfield.org/stargospel.html

[43] *Is There A Gospel in the Stars* (2014, February 19). Retrieved from http://www.setterfield.org/stargospel.html

Virgo's legs and is the largest or chief planet of our solar system, known as the King planet[44], representing Christ, the King (Isaiah 9:6). So in the stars we see exactly what John saw. A woman clothed in the sun with the moon at her feet and a garland or crown of twelve stars above her head, travailing in pain as she gives birth.

[44] *Zedek* (2014, February 19). Retrieved from http://www.varchive. org/itb/zedek.htm

Amazingly, the story in the stars does not end here. There is another facet to the great sign that demonstrates God's handiwork in the heavens and that adds even more credibility to this being the great sign John saw. As with any birth, there is a pregnancy. Let's take a look using Stellarium to see the movement of the sun, moon, stars, and wandering stars (planets)[45] unfold day by day.

The search for the pregnancy begins with placing the following date in the date and time box: 2016 11 30 (year, month, day). When you do this, you will see Jupiter has already entered Virgo's womb. Jupiter moves around in Virgo's womb until 2017 09 09. Jupiter is then birthed, moving down between Virgo's legs from 2017 09 09 to 2017 09 23, when the moon drops to Virgo's feet.

So let's do the math. Jupiter was in Virgo's womb from November 30, 2016 to September 9, 2017, which is a total of nine months and ten days (280 days). This is in line with the length of time of a typical pregnancy, which lasts 38–40 weeks or 266–280 days, respectively[46].

This is so astounding. Truly God is showing His handiwork in the stars, his billboard, as His stars are for signs. Are we listening to God's signs? Are we

---

[45] *Wandering Star* (2014, February 19). http://en.wikipedia.org/wiki/ Wandering_star

[46] Cavendish, M. (1998). Encyclopedia of Family Health. In M. Cavendish, *Encyclopedia of Family Health* (p. 1477). New York: Marshall Cavendish Corporation.

paying attention to ascertain their meaning(s)? Are we spiritually prepared, ready, awake and watching?

So what is so great about this great sign? I believe it is "the key" to unlocking end times Bible prophecy with regard to the rapture of the bride of Christ, the beginning of the tribulation period, and the second coming of Christ, ending the tribulation period. This is a very bold statement indeed. The implications of this are indeed sobering, as we have no excuse for not being ready for our Bridegroom. We must have sufficient oil in our lamps. We must be spiritually prepared, ready, awake, and watching and ready at a moment's notice for a shout and blasting of a trumpet, heralding the return of the Bridegroom for His bride.

After the great sign, John saw another sign in heaven. A fiery red Dragon (Satan) is thrown to earth with the dragon's tail drawing a third of the angels in heaven with him. This is not a heavenly sign from the perspective of being seen in the stars, but is actually Satan and his angels being physically thrown to earth, having no more access to heaven where he has made accusations against us before God day and night (Revelation 12:10). Satan, knowing his time is short, begins to persecute the woman (Israel), which gave birth to Christ (Revelation 12:13). The woman then flees to the wilderness where God protects her for 1,260 days (Revelation 12:14–16). These three signs come in rapid succession at the end of the "minor" tribulation or the

end of the first 1,260 days. The first sign of the woman
is played out in the stars. Soon after that, the sign of
the fiery red Dragon is a physical event with Satan
being thrown to earth. This leads to the second actual
physical event occurring on earth with the dragon
(Satan) pursuing the woman (Nation of Israel; Jewish
people) into the wilderness where God protects her for
1,260 days.

Additionally, in the great sign there are two
constellations, Virgo and Leo, which are the first and
last constellations in the Mazzaroth[47]. The Mazzaroth
contains the twelve constellations (zodiac), outlining
God's redemptive plan for humankind. This reminds
me of Christ declaring that He is the alpha and omega
(Revelation 1:8; 21:6), the beginning and the end. It's
interesting that these two constellations would be
together during the tribulation. Let's briefly examine the
Mazzaroth, because the firmament is Gods handiwork,
declaring the glory of God, speaking to humankind
unto the ends of the world (Psalm 19:1–4) so that we
have no excuse for not acknowledging God, the Creator
(Romans 1:18–20). God placed the stars in the heavens
to speak to humankind with regard to divide the day
from the night, signs, divine appointments (festivals,
feasts), and for days and years (Genesis 1:14).

---

[47] Unknown. (2014, February 17). *Mazzaroth - Wikipedia, the free
encyclopedia.* Retrieved from Mazzaroth: http://en.wikipedia.org/
wiki/Mazzaroth

Chapter 8

THE MAZZAROTH

The term *Mazzaroth* appears one time in the oldest book in the Bible, the book of Job, and is meant to be understood as the movement of the constellations in their season (Job 38:32). The Mazzaroth consists of twelve constellations that are also known today as the zodiac. From beginning to end, they are Virgo, Libra, Scorpio, Sagittarius, Capricorn, Aquarius, Pisces, Aries, Taurus, Gemini, Cancer, and Leo. These twelve constellations tell a story with regard to Jesus Christ's redemptive plan for humankind.

The first constellation in the Mazzaroth is Virgo, which is depicted as a woman holding ears of wheat in her left hand and a branch in her right hand. Virgo represents the virgin who gives birth to the Messiah as prophesied (Genesis 3:15), affirmed (Isaiah 7:14), and fulfilled in the Old Testament (by prophecy and affirmation) and New Testament (the actual fulfillment) (Matthew 21:22–23).

The second constellation is Libra, which is depicted as a set of scales or balances with one side being lower than the other. Libra represents Christ's necessary redemptive sacrifice (death) for humankind—His life being the price paid for humankind's sin and its subsequent need for redemption. Though He was sinless, Christ, being falsely accused, was weighed on the balances and sacrificed Himself willingly for the sins of humankind as the lamb without blemish.

The third constellation is Scorpio, which is depicted as a scorpion. Scorpio represents Christ's trials while on earth—Christ resisting temptation through all attempts by Satan to cause Him to sin. It's a picture of Christ's trials here on earth, as a scorpion inflicts pain. Christ is the only person who ever lived a life without sin, being righteous unto His death, thus defeating Satan.

The fourth constellation is Sagittarius, which is depicted as an archer with the upper body of a man and the lower body of a horse. He holds a bow in his hands with an arrow pointing directly at the heart of Scorpio while the archer stands on Draco's head. The centaur has two natures, just as Christ had two natures, God and human, representing Christ's victory over Satan. Though Satan bruised Christ's heel in Christ's sinless death, Christ crushed Satan's head, defeating Satan through His virgin birth, sinless life as a man and as God, and his subsequent death, burial, and resurrection.

The fifth constellation is Capricorn, which is depicted as a sea goat, half fish and half goat. The sea goat denotes a sacrificial goat coming from the sea (which represents humankind in Bible prophecy [Revelation 13:1]) of humanity. The goat was a sacrificial animal in Jewish culture with two roles to play. One goat was a scapegoat, carrying the people's sin into the wilderness (Leviticus 16:10). The other goat was sacrificed on the altar as a sin offering to God (Leviticus 16:9). Christ fulfilled both purposes, taking up our infirmities and carrying our sorrows as the Son of Man who came out of the sea of humanity (Isaiah 53:4–5).

The sixth constellation is Aquarius, which is depicted as a man holding a two-handled pitcher with water being poured out to two fish below him. Aquarius represents Christ pouring living waters (John 4:14) to the fish (Pisces). This a perfect picture of Christ giving living waters to those He receives unto himself.

The seventh constellation is Pisces, which is depicted by two fish, one in a horizontal and one in a vertical position, bound together by a band at their tails. Pisces is a picture of two multitudes who are being blessed, representing Israel being the earthly or horizontal fish, and the vertical fish being comprised of the body of believing Christians who are receiving life-giving eternal waters from Christ who is standing above the fish as the water bearer[48]. A fish symbol was used by Christians in Christ's time and is defined by the Greek term ΙΧΘΥΣ, which is a Greek acrostic or acronym that translates to English as "Jesus Christ, God's Son, Savior."[49]

The eighth constellation is Aries, which is depicted as a ram or a lamb trampling and breaking the bands attaching the fish to an ominous sea monster (Cetus). Cetus is a scaly-headed monster with a whale's body that would devour the two fish, who are tied to it through sin. So in this picture we see Christ, who takes away the sin of the world (John 1:29) after being broken for us (1 Corinthians 11:24), trampling and breaking the sin-bond between Satan and humankind, for both Jew and Gentile who would receive Him.

The ninth constellation is Taurus, which is depicted as a charging bull. This constellation includes the two star clusters Pleiades and Hyades. The bull symbolizes Christ as a redeemer (John 19:37; Isaiah 44:24) of Israel and as a mighty warrior at his second coming (Isaiah 1:24–28; 34:2–8; 44:6–7, 22–23; 49:26; Jeremiah 31:10–11; Zechariah 12:9–10; Hebrews 10:13–14; Revelation 1:7). The bull or ox was the biggest and most costly of all the sacrifices, symbolizing great wealth due to good

[48] Unknown. (2014, 02 17). *Gospel in the Stars*. Retrieved from Is there a Gospel in the Stars: http://www.setterfield.org/stargospel.html

[49] Unknown. (2014, 04 13). *Wikipedia the Free Encyclopedia*. Retrieved from Ichthys: http://en.wikipedia.org/wiki/Ichthys

times or great prosperity (Isaiah 30:23–24; 32:20). It symbolized Jesus Christ, who gave up His riches to become a man and pay for the sins of the world (2 Corinthians 8:9; Philippians 2:6–8).

The tenth constellation is Gemini, which is depicted as two people, male and female. This constellation symbolizes Christ returning with His bride during His second coming at the end of the Great Tribulation (Revelation 19:6–16).

The eleventh constellation is Cancer, which is depicted as a crab. As many animals do, crabs molt when they grow, changing smaller shells for larger ones. With the crab's growth, the crab becomes ever bigger and stronger in a better body. This is a picture of Christians who put off their old ways for those of eternal life (Ephesians 4:24).

The twelfth, and final, constellation is Leo, depicted as a lion with a serpent underfoot ridden by a crow (Crovus) and bowl (Crater). This constellation depicts two things. First, the crow depicts the birds that will eat the flesh of Satan's armies (Revelation 19:17–18) after the cup of God's wrath has been poured out upon an unrepentant humankind during the great tribulation (Revelation 14:10; 16:19). Second, Christ is depicted as the lion of the Tribe of Judah treading underfoot the Serpent, the Enemy that bruised Christ's heel as He returns during His second coming at the end of the great tribulation. The brightest star in this constellation is Regulus[50], from which we get the term *regal*.[51] So the Mazzaroth as written in the stars begins with Christ's Virgin birth and ends in His victorious return to earth as King of Kings and Lord of Lords (Revelation 19:16); he returns as a lion, not a lamb, warring with unrepentant humankind and the Antichrist.

[50] *Is There A Gospel in the Stars* (2014, February 19). Retrieved from http://www.setterfield.org/stargospel.html

[51] *Is There A Gospel in the Stars* (2014, February 19). Retrieved from http://www.setterfield.org/stargospel.html

Chapter 9

BIBLE PROPHECY—HE WANTS US TO KNOW

I came to know Christ many years ago, as even as a young child, I marveled at God's creation, the variety of the animals and plants. These spoke to me, suggesting that there was a Creator. I didn't buy in to the theory of evolution based on embryonic stages of development shown in my science classes. And that's all evolution is—a theory with no scientific evidence based on facts. I found it more plausible to believe a divine Creator was responsible for what I saw on earth and in the heavens that surrounded me. Once I accepted Christ as my Savior, I wanted to know Him more and obtain a deeper relationship with Him. Through this process, I sought additional biblical evidence to support what I believe beyond God creating the heavens and the earth and all of God's creation on the earth. I found what I wanted. More exactly, I found what I needed in biblical prophecy.

Biblical prophecy separates Christianity from all other religions. In fact, God specifically states that there is no other, none like Him, and that He makes known the end from the beginning, from ancient of times and from what still is to come (Isaiah 46:9–10). So God knows all things and has chosen to make known to us, through the Bible, the prophetic events before they happen. No other book does this. In fact, the God of the Bible challenges all those who worship idols and other gods of this world and their corresponding religious systems. God says to them, present their case and set forth their arguments. He then advises them to bring in their idols of wood and stone to tell us what is going to happen, and to tell us what the former things were, so that we may consider them and know their final ending. God finally asks them that their idols declare to us future events, telling us what the future holds, so that we may know that these idols are gods (Isaiah 41:21–23). God issued this challenge because He knows there is no God but Him. Therefore, it stands to reason that He is the only One who can with 100 percent accuracy declare events before they happen, declaring the final outcome from the beginning. Consequently, we are also exhorted by Peter to rely on biblical prophecies and pay attention to them, even as a light that shines in a dark place (2 Peter 1:19). Peter goes on to emphasize that no prophecy came about by the prophet's own interpretation but only to write those things God has revealed at the leading of the Holy Spirit (2 Peter 1:20–21).

I contend that the Old Testament declared Christ's first coming with prophecies of His birth, ministry, death, and resurrection. Why is this important? Because God wanted us to know His Son was coming and for us to have no excuse for not recognizing Christ for who He was and is, the Son of God. Additionally, if it was important enough to God to provide sufficient prophetic detail for us to recognize Christ's first coming, then why wouldn't Christ provide sufficient detail about when the rapture of the church and Christ's second coming, when His feet touches the Mount of Olives? The fact is that Christ does provide sufficient detail for both of these. God the Father then shows the great sign to John, which then provides the context for the rapture of Christ's bride. Why all the prophetic details? Again, God and Christ want us to know so that we have no excuse. We, Christians, are exhorted to be diligent, to show ourselves approved unto God, rightly dividing the word of truth. So first, let's examine what the Old Testament says about Christ's birth, ministry, death, and resurrection.

In the Old Testament where Christ is concealed, many prophecies and events herald the coming of a Messiah. Let's first take a look at Passover. After the nation of Israel left Egypt, God commanded Israel to observe Passover, wherein an animal without blemish was slain once a year to atone for someone's sins. This is a picture of Christ being slain for our sins. So if Christ was slain on Passover, He would immediately be buried before the Sabbath during the Feast of Unleavened Bread. Christ was then prophesied in the Old Testament to rise after three days (Hosea 6:2), which would be during the Feast of Firstfruits, as Christ is the firstfruit of those who believe in Him. Christ being the Passover Lamb is further supported when God tells Abraham to take his only son, Isaac, to Moriah where Abraham is to sacrifice him as a burnt offering on the mountains there (Genesis 2:2). Here, God is testing Abraham to see if he would obey God even to the point of not withholding his only son. God had no intention to make Abraham sacrifice Isaac and provided a ram caught in a thicket as the burnt offering (Genesis 22:13). This is the picture of God not withholding His only Son, Jesus Christ, who was to be sacrificed for humankind's sin.

The Old Testament contains at least 100 prophecies, some of which were written hundreds of years before fulfillment, relating to Jesus' birth, death, and resurrection. Why so many? Could it be that God did not want us to miss this divine appointment with His Son, Jesus Christ? God wanted us to know for sure who He was. In fact, Jesus Himself rebuked the Pharisees and Sadducees for knowing how to discern the weather but unable to discern the signs of the times with regard to Christ's first appearance on earth (Matthew 16:1-4). God took such great lengths through biblical prophecy to highlight His son's birth, death, and resurrection because He wants us to know who Christ really is, the Son of God, so that we would not have any excuse for not recognizing Christ.

There are at least thirty Old Testament prophetical references regarding Christ's birth and forty-eight New Testament references of Christ fulfilling all the Old Testament references. These are a few of the Old Testament references regarding Christ's birth. Christ was prophesied to be born as an eternal (Micah 5:2) firstborn son (Exodus 13:2; Numbers 3:13; 8:17) of a virgin (Isaiah 7:13-14), from the seed of the woman (Genesis 3:15). He was to be born of the Tribe of Judah (Genesis 49:8-10; Micah 5:2) in the line of Abraham (Genesis 26:3-4; 17:7-8), Isaac (Genesis 17:19; 21:12; 26:2-4), Jacob (Genesis 28:13-14; Numbers 24:17,19) and David (2 Samuel 7:12-13; Isaiah 9:7; Jeremiah 23:5; 30:9) as a king (2 Samuel 7:12-13; Isaiah 9:7; Jeremiah 23:5; 30:9) in the town of Bethlehem of Judea (Micah 5:2-5). Additional Old Testament prophecies relating to Christ's birth mention that kings would bring Him gifts, falling down before Him (Psalm 72:10-11) and the massacre of many children (Jeremiah 31:15). All of these references were fulfilled by Christ as detailed in the New Testament, as He is the eternal (John 1:1,

4; 8:58; Colossians 1:15–19) firstborn son (Luke 2:7, 23)
born of a virgin (Matthew 1:18–23; Luke 1:27–35) from
the seed of the woman (Galatians 4:4; Hebrews 2:14;
1 John 3:8), born of the Tribe of Judah (Matthew 1:2-3;
Hebrews 7:14 ; Revelation 5:5) in the line of Abraham
(Matthew 1:1, 17; Galatians 3:16), Isaac (Matthew 1:2,
17; Romans 9:7; Hebrews 11:17–19), Jacob (Matthew
1:2; Luke 1:33; 3:23–38), and David as a king (Matthew
1:1, 6; 9:27; 12:22–23; 15:22; 20:30–31; 21:9, 15; 22:41–42;
Luke 1:32; John 18:36–37; Acts 13:22–23) in the town of
Bethlehem of Judea (Matthew 2:1-6; Luke 2:4-11). As
we all know, the kings of the east brought Christ gifts
and fell down before Him (Matthew 2:1–11), and Herod
massacred many children in an attempt to kill Christ
(Matthew 2:16–18).

Similarly, at least fifty Old Testament prophecies
concern Christ's death and resurrection are fulfilled
in the New Testament, further validating Christ as the
Son of God. Again, through the Holy Spirit, God told
to the Old Testament prophets the many prophecies
concerning Jesus Christ so that we would know He is
the Son of God. So, if God took so much effort to provide
the prophetical signposts for His Son's first coming
so that we couldn't miss it, it only seems reasonable
that He would provide the necessary signposts for the
bride's rapture and Christ's second coming.

Let's look at what the New Testament says regarding
these two events.

Christ prophesied in the New Testament about the timing of His bride's rapture and God, through the apostle John, spoke of His Son's second coming, as Christ did not want us to miss the rapture. God also wanted to show His divine prophetical omniscience by showing the prophet Daniel the exact timing of Christ's second coming. Christ spoke to the Christian disciples who were also Jews practicing the Lord's feasts about the rapture of His bride. So, when Christ told them He would return at an unknown day and hour at the last trumpet, He was using an idiom for the Feast of Trumpets (Matthew 13:32). The prophet Daniel wrote of the exact number of days with regard to Christ's second coming, detailing the exact time period when the Antichrist signs the seven-year peace covenant to Christ's second coming (Daniel 9:7).

Chapter 10

PUTTING THE PIECES TOGETHER

L et's review. As previously discussed, Christ fulfilled the Jewish spring feasts and He will fulfill the Jewish fall feasts. Based on Jewish tradition, customs, and practice, the Feast of Trumpets will be the time of the rapture of the bride of Christ. The book of Revelation is chronological in nature with the great sign appearing at the end of the "minor" tribulation period (first 1,260 days).

Now let's chart what we know based on NASA's blood moon tetrad forecast and the Stellarium's date of the great sign. The chart below depicts the four blood moons of 2014 and 2015, solar eclipse, and the great sign pointing toward an unknown timeline with regard to end time events. This enables the timeline to unfold based on future prophetic events as detailed in the book of Revelation—and the entire Bible for that matter. At the top of the chart is the fulfillment of the spring feasts and future unfulfilled fall feasts.

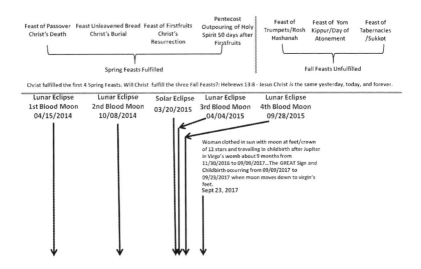

Now we've mapped the dates for the signs with their specific dates for the four blood moons, solar eclipse, and the great sign, we must determine what is next to be mapped on the timeline. If the great sign (the key) is at the end of the "minor" tribulation period or first 1,260 days, what is the Day of Atonement (Yom Kippur) about 1,260 days from 9/23/2017 (the great sign)? After looking at many websites, there appears to be a spread of dates for Yom Kippur/the Day of Atonement consisting of September 16, 2014[52], September 28, 2021[53],

---

[52] Unknown. (2014, 02 23). *Jewish Holy Day and Festival Calendar - 2012-2021 (5772-5782)*. Retrieved from http://www.njgsc.org/Jewish-Calendar-2012-2021.pdf

[53] Unknown. (2014, 02 23). *Congregation Shir Hadash*. Retrieved from Jewish Holidays 5781: http://www.shirhadash.org/calendar/holidays.cgi?y=2021+ce

and October 17, 2021.[54] So I will just use the spread of September–October 2021. In any case, the date for the Day of Atonement should be after the autumnal equinox (September 22, 2021[55]) as a fall feast should occur in the fall, rather than the hot days of summer. Therefore, I will use the nonspecific date of September–October 2021 as the date for Yom Kippur. A specific date is not necessary here, as general spread of about thirty days in the September–October timeframe is sufficient. As Christ fulfilled the spring feasts, Christ will fulfill the fall feasts. This is the first Yom Kippur that occurs approximately 1,260 days after the great sign. Let's go back to the chart and add what we now know, updating this latest signpost.

---

[54] Unknown. (2014, 02 23). *Projected Appointed Times for 2001 - 2030* . Retrieved from http://www.truthontheweb.org/AT2010.htm

[55] Unknown. (2014, February 23). *TorahCalendar.com*. Retrieved from Month 7 Spiritual Year 6007: http://www.torahcalendar.com/Calendar.asp?YM=Y2021M7

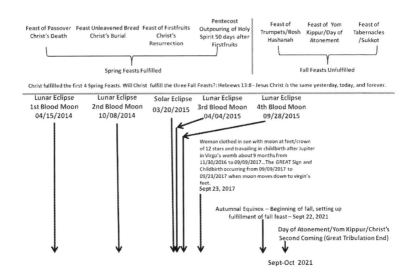

Now let's examine the Bible for additional clues so we can continue to build the timeline of the end times. Because of the chronological timeframe of the book of Revelation, we know that after the great sign, Satan will be thrown to earth and pursue the woman into the wilderness where she will be protected by God for 1,260 days. Based on these prophetic signposts, let's go back to the chart, moving backwards 1,260 days to when the woman flees in to the wilderness and is held there securely by God. After moving back 1,260 days from September–October 2021, we get April–May 2018. So, the woman will be protected by God during the April–May, 2018 timeframe with 1,260 days of God's protection from roughly this date to September–October 2021. Let's update the chart with this additional signposts.

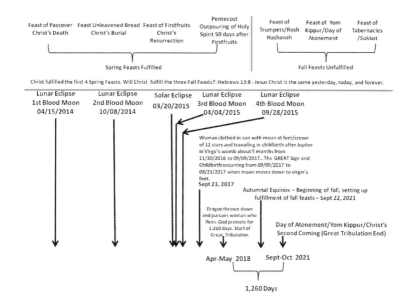

Now let's continue to examine the Bible for additional clues to build our timeline. Because of the timeframe of the book of Revelation, we know that after the great sign, Satan will be thrown to earth and pursue the woman into the wilderness. As the tribulation is 2,520 days, we know her fleeing into the wilderness marks the end of the first half of this period. So, again, counting back 1,260 days will give us the start date for the tribulation when the Antichrist signs a seven-year covenant with Israel, which is October–November 2014. Let's update the chart again with his new information.

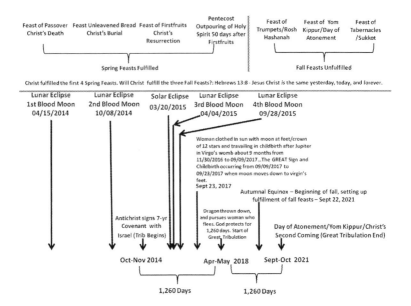

We are still not done. Due to the chronological timeframe of the book of Revelation, we know that Christ fulfills the rapture of the church, Christ's bride, on the Feast of Trumpets before the start of the tribulation period. So, what is the last Feast of Trumpets before this time? This feast encompasses two days, from the evening of September 25, 2014 to sunset on September 27, 2014[56]. Additionally, this is a fall feast, so let's make sure the autumnal equinox occurs before

---

[56] Fairchild, M. (2014, 02 23). *About.com Christianity*. Retrieved from Bible Feasts Calendar 2013-2017 Dates of Jewish Holidays and Feasts in the Bible: http://christianity.about.com/od/biblefactsandlists/a/biblefeastscal.htm

this date, which it does on September 23, 2014[57]—two days before the start of the Feast of Trumpets, which is spot-on, the way it is supposed to be! Again, let's update the chart.

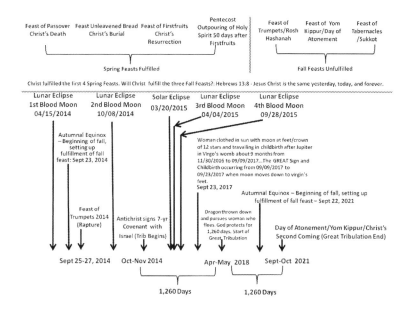

Now let's take a look at the upcoming four blood moons in context with our chart. What do you see? It's clear that the first two blood moons occur before the rapture and the Antichrist's signing of the seven-year covenant, beginning the tribulation. These moons serve as omens or warnings to the nation of Israel. The solar eclipse, two remaining blood moons, and the great

[57] Unknown. (2014, February 23). *TorahCalendar.com*. Retrieved from Month 6 spiritual Year 6000: http://www.torahcalendar.com/Calendar.asp?PYM=Y2014M6

sign appear as warnings to the nations of the earth and Israel, respectively, heralding the great tribulation. Just as in the previous three blood moon tetrads, there will be tears for the nation of Israel with regard to the abomination of desolation and Israel fleeing in to the wilderness where God will protect Her. Then there will be a great victory when Israel acknowledges its offense and her people turn their hearts toward Christ, saying, "Blessed is He who comes in the name of the Lord" (Revelation 1:8; 21:6).

It's amazing that the Feast of Trumpets is a time of repentance that calls for great introspection and preparation to meet God at His judgment seat on the Day of Atonement (Christ's second coming). This is exactly what the tribulation is about for those who are left behind, Jew and Gentile alike. All of God's seal, trumpet, and bowl judgments are not to slay an unrepentant humanity but bring them to repentance and God's saving grace for the meeting with Him at the Day of Atonement. This will be partially realized in the Nation of Israel during the tribulation period as two-thirds of the population will die during this time (Zechariah 13:8-9). Having said that, the remnant will turn toward Christ, for Christ says He will not return until the Jewish people recognize Him as their Savior. This is found in the following verses:

O Jerusalem, Jerusalem, the one who kills the prophets and stones those who are sent to her! How often I wanted to gather your children together, as a hen gathers her chicks under her wings, but you were not willing! See! Your house is left to you desolate; for I say to you, you shall see Me no more till you say, "Blessed is He who comes in the name of the Lord!" (Matthew 23:37–39)

I will return again to My place till they acknowledge their offense. Then they will seek My face; In their affliction they will earnestly seek Me. (Hosea 5:15)

Come, and let us return to the Lord; For He has torn, but He will heal us; He has stricken, but He will bind us up. After two days He will revive us; on the third day He will raise us up, that we may live in His sight. Let us know, let us pursue the knowledge of the Lord. His going forth is established as the morning; He will come to us like the rain, like the latter and former rain to the earth. (Hosea 6:1–3)

And I will pour on the house of David and on the inhabitants of Jerusalem the Spirit of grace and supplication; then they will look on Me whom they pierced. Yes, they will mourn for Him as

one mourns for his only son, and grieve for Him
as one grieves for a firstborn. (Zechariah 12:10)

However, this is not true of the Gentiles for the
most part. Instead of humankind repenting, mankind
is deceived by the Antichrist, hardens its heart toward
God, and remains unrepentant, according to the
following verses:

> But the rest of mankind, who were not killed
> by these plagues, did not repent of the works
> of their hands, that they should not worship
> demons, and idols of gold, silver, brass, stone,
> and wood, which can neither see nor hear nor
> walk. (Revelation 9:20)

> And they did not repent of their murders or
> their sorceries or their sexual immorality or their
> thefts. (Revelation 9:21)

> And men were scorched with great heat, and
> they blasphemed the name of God who has
> power over these plagues; and they did not
> repent and give Him glory. (Revelation 16:9)

> They blasphemed the God of heaven because of
> their pains and their sores, and did not repent of
> their deeds. (Revelation 16:11)

In fact, humankind's hatred for God will be so intense that when Christ appears with His angel armies and His bride, humankind is still not only unrepentant but warlike against Him.

> And I saw the beast, the kings of the earth, and their armies, gathered together to make war against Him who sat on the horse and against His army. (Revelation 19:19)

Ultimately, Christ conquers these unrepentant nations and peoples. The Antichrist is also captured.

> And the armies in heaven, clothed in fine linen, white and clean, followed Him on white horses. Now out of His mouth goes a sharp sword, that with it He should strike the nations. And He Himself will rule them with a rod of iron. He Himself treads the winepress of the fierceness and wrath of Almighty God. (Revelation 19:14–15)

> Then the beast was captured, and with him the false prophet who worked signs in his presence, by which he deceived those who received the mark of the beast and those who worshiped his image. (Revelation 19–20)

Chapter 11

Watchman on the Wall

Recently, Pastor Hagee wrote a book, *Four Blood Moons: Something is About to Change* (Worthy Publishing, October 2013), highlighting the historical significance of the three previous blood moon tetrads that occurred on Passover and Tabernacles. Evangelist Perry Stone also recently released a book, *The Prophetic Future Concealed in Israel's Festivals*. He discussed the book recently on Sid Roth's *It's Supernatural*, detailing the Lord's feasts and their relevance to Bible prophecy.

I agree with both these men of God that the four blood moons are significant signposts and that Israel's feasts are God's prophetic divine appointments. However, the great sign provides the additional context needed for the four blood moons and the Lord's fall feasts, making them even more relevant to the time in which we are living. Something is definitely about to change, and now we know when.

I wrote this book with great confidence that the great sign as depicted in the Stellarium software is the great sign in revelation 12:1. The great sign appears on 09/23/2017 during the day at the very end of the "minor" tribulation period. This great sign doesn't occur in the next 100 years and beyond. Also, it doesn't occur from present day to 09/22/2017. In fact, this alignment happened only one time for the generation that saw the rebirth of Israel (05/14/1948) and for the generation that saw the Jewish people take back total control of Jerusalem (Six-Day War, June 6–10, 1967).

This book is based on the great sign being "the key" to unlocking the end times. I, as a Watchman on the Wall, am obligated to warn not only the Christian community but nonbelievers as well. This is the best way to do that. Many will say that I am date setting. However, it would be an egregious mistake for me to not warn others as the age of grace of the church age rapidly comes to a close. I have never set any dates before; however, the evidence is so overwhelming that this Watchman on the Wall has to give a clarion cry to all who will listen, helping ensure as many Christians as possible are spiritually prepared, ready, awake, and watching for Christ's return. This is not date setting but recognizing the dates of the four blood moons as indicated by NASA and the date of the great sign as indicated by the Stellarium software. I wrote this book knowing there will be those who cannot help themselves in condemning what I have done. However, I would implore them to build up instead of tear down. I need everyone's support to help warn others as time is rapidly ticking down toward the harvest of the bride when the bride of Christ will be raptured on the Feast of Trumpets in the twinkling of an eye at the last trump with a shout.

There is no excuse for not being ready. I think God wants it that way as there is so much at stake. Christ is at the door and knocking. Can you hear Him?

Chapter 12

LOOKING AHEAD–WHAT NOW?

Wow! Now that you are aware of the rapidly approaching coming of the Bridegroom and the rapture of His bride, what are you going to do about it? If you are a believer, ensure there is plenty of oil in your lamp; be spiritually prepared, ready, awake, and watching for the Bridegroom's heralded return. Also, tell others. Become a Watchman on the Wall who sounds the alarm, ensuring your friends, family, and others are spiritually prepared for this momentous worldwide event that will leave this world in chaos and confusion in the twinkling of an eye, ripe for the Antichrist's great deception (2 Thessalonians 2:11) as God will not be mocked (Galatians 6:7). The atheists or God deniers and God haters who continually push the boundaries of human behavior away from God will finally get the world they want, a world without God where 50 percent of humankind will die as detailed in the following verses:

> Then two men will be in the field: one will be taken and the other left. Two women will be grinding at the mill: one will be taken and the other left. (Matthew 24:40–41)

> So I looked, and behold, a pale horse. And the name of him who sat on it was Death, and Hades followed with him. And power was given to them over a fourth of the earth, to kill with sword, with hunger, with death, and by the beasts of the earth. (Revelation 6:8)

> Then the sixth angel sounded: And I heard a voice from the four horns of the golden altar which is before God, saying to the sixth angel who had the trumpet, "Release the four angels who are bound at the great river Euphrates." So the four angels, who had been prepared for the hour and day and month and year, were released to kill a third of mankind. (Revelation 9:13–15)

Let's do the math regarding the 50 percent of humankind who will die during the tribulation. Let's say that after the rapture six billion people will remain on the earth. If one-third of humankind is killed as described in Revelation 6:8, then four billion people remain. Then if one-fourth of the four billion of humankind is killed in Revelation 9:13–15, that leaves three billion or 50 percent. Many think Matthew 24:40–41 is about the rapture. It's not, because it would denote that 50 percent of mankind will be raptured. This is just not the case as the number will be much smaller with 50 percent of Christians being raptured as Christ's bride as previously discussed in the Parable of the Ten Virgins.

It makes me sick when I hear comedians and talk show hosts or anyone for that matter ridiculing Christians and God to just get a few laughs. No one will be laughing when the rapture occurs and all those left behind will be subjected to the Antichrist's great deception (2 Thessalonians 2:11). No one will be laughing at the great white throne Judgment where all nonbelievers will be thrown in to the lake of fire, with wailing and gnashing of their teeth as stated in the following Bible verses:

Then I saw a great white throne and Him who sat on it, from whose face the earth and the heaven fled away. And there was found no place for them. And I saw the dead, small and great, standing before God, and books were opened. And another book was opened, which is the Book of Life. And the dead were judged according to their works, by the things which were written in the books. The sea gave up the dead who were in it, and Death and Hades delivered up the dead who were in them. And they were judged, each one according to his works. Then Death and Hades were cast into the lake of fire. This is the second death. And anyone not found written in the Book of Life was cast into the lake of fire. (Revelation 20:11–15)

Again, the kingdom of heaven is like a dragnet that was cast into the sea and gathered some of every kind, which, when it was full, they drew to shore; and they sat down and gathered the good into vessels, but threw the bad away. So it will be at the end of the age. The angels will come forth, separate the wicked from among the just, and cast them into the furnace of fire. There will be wailing and gnashing of teeth. (Matthew 13:47–50)

If you are a nonbeliever, now is the time to become a believer in Christ, a Christian. For no one comes to the Father but through Christ (John 14:6). The time is so short. The window on the age of grace is closing. You do not need to "fix yourself" before asking Jesus Christ to forgive you of your sins no matter how bad you think they are. That's the beauty of Christ's unconditional love. Come as you are. There is no sin you have ever committed that Christ cannot or will not forgive. You are not alone. All have sinned and come short of the glory of God (Romans 3:23). To be saved, believe in Christ (Acts 16:31) having died on the cross to save you from your sins and confess those sins, and Christ will be faithful to forgive you for your sins (1 John 1:9). A simple prayer to Christ, the King of Kings and Lord of Lords, is all it takes. Christ is ever-ready to receive your prayer.

A simple prayer you may want to use to help you toward the narrow path of eternal life, light, and freedom from sin and eternal suffering is as follows:

Dear Jesus, I am a sinner. I need You as my Savior.
Please come in to my life and forgive me of my sins.
Let my life be renewed in You, that
I may serve and live for You.
You are now my Hope, my Comforter,
my Strength and my Lord.

I hope you have made the right decision to follow Christ. If you have decided to accept Him as your Savior, that decision is the most important one you have made or will ever make in your life. The angels in heaven are rejoicing (Luke 15:10) for you for having the faith to trust in Jesus, making Him the foundational cornerstone (Ephesians 2:20) of your new life in Him. Rest now in the comfort of knowing that you have the

King of Kings and the Lord of Lords (Revelation 19:16) on your side. He will never leave you or forsake you (Deuteronomy 31:8). Welcome to the Kingdom of God. Watch and pray always that you are worthy to escape all those things that are about to come upon the earth and stand before Christ (Luke 21:36). Now help warn your friends, family, and others as time is so short. It's an exciting time to be alive!